SIPPING FEAR PISSING CONFIDENCE

For Men: Solving the Riddle of Your Addictions

Christopher K Wallace

ISBN 978-1-987954-05-0 Library and Archives Canada

SIPPING FEAR PISSING CONFIDENCE

For Men: Solving the Riddle of Your Addictions

CHRISTOPHER K WALLACE

copyright Christopher K Wallace and ckerbooks.com, 2022

All rights reserved. No part of this publication may be reproduced, distributed, transmitted in any form or by any means, including photocopying, recording, or other electronic methods, without the prior written permission of the author, except in the case of brief quotations embodied in critical reviews and certain other non-commercial uses permitted by copyright law.

ISBN 978-1-987954-05-0 Library and Archives Canada

Cover design by Designsware

Sketches by Theramses

Portions of this book drew on ideas appearing in *Drinkers' Riddle*, 2015, published by

CK Wallace and ckerbooks.com

Christopher K Wallace, BST, CH*

advisortomen.com

* available for speaking, podcasts, etc.

Why Read This Book

Addictions involve narrowing focus to relieve stress. Discover how desire is a form of fear. Just like many others, learn how to use this to overcome any addiction.

Christopher K Wallace is a behavioural science trained counsellor and hypnotist focusing on mental fitness as the advisor to men. He has a colourful past and uses his experience to help men reclaim their power and use it in service of themselves and others to find meaning and freedom. He does free calls for men and sometimes agrees to work with them. Find him at advisortomen.com

ISBN 978-1-987954-05-0 Library and Archives Canada

Dedicated to all the unforgettable souls lost to fear addiction...

SIPPING FEAR, PISSING CONFIDENCE

Table of Contents

Introduction 1

PART ONE: THE RIDDLE : 5
Riddle: a puzzling fact, thing, or person…

1. CRUX 7
   Crux Introduction 7
   Crux Talk 8
   Crux Bamboozle 11
2. CONFIDENCE 17
   Confidence Displacement 17
   Learned Helplessness 18
   Building Confidence 19
3. WANTING 24
   Wanting and Suffering 24
   Wanting and Fear 26
   Wanting Suffering Cycle 27
4. WINNING 30
   Free Will 30
   Confronting Wanting 31
   Defending Confidence 34
5. TESTING 39
   Relapse 39
   Triggers and Consequences 40
   Testing for Abstinence 43
6. CAGING 48
   Body Thoughts 48
   Caging the Wolf 52
   Claiming Identity 54
7. CHOSEN 58
   Chosen 58
   Soul and Spirit 60
   Purpose 62

PART TWO: THE TWIDDLE ... 67
Twiddle: a series of small twists and turns...

8. TRAUMA ... 69
    - Guilt ... 69
    - Shame ... 71
    - Trauma ... 73
9. EMOTIONS ... 79
    - Constructed Emotion ... 79
    - The Crazy 8 ... 83
    - Universal Love ... 85
10. DEPRESSION ... 89
    - Normal Depression ... 89
    - Meds, Renewal, and The Hero's Journey ... 91
    - Re-Purpose ... 94
11. ANXIETY ... 98
    - Describing Anxiety ... 98
    - The Attachment Threat Cycle ... 101
    - Countering Strategies ... 105
12. STRESS ... 110
    - General Adaptation Syndrome ... 110
    - Nervous System Training ... 112
    - Fear Seeker ... 116
13. LOVE ... 123
    - Oedipal Male ... 123
    - Life Cycles ... 125
    - Masculine Maturity ... 128
14. NEEDS ... 132
    - The Six Human Needs ... 132
    - Positive vs Negative ... 135
    - Relationship Needs ... 137
Conclusion ... 144
    - Sex Differences ... 145
    - Addiction Peculiarities ... 149
    - Nervous Capitalism ... 154
RESOURCES ... 161
APPENDIX A ... 170
APPENDIX B ... 173

Introduction

Let me begin by explaining the title's reference to fear. Survival is paramount for each of us, and so there is a fear for every context.

According to my dad's Gage Canadian Dictionary the word fear is "an unpleasant emotion caused by exposure to danger." But it can also be "anxiety for the safety of" and includes having a fearful respect and being fearful of danger; add in being fearful of the likelihood of something or being afraid of something, as in fear of failure or fear of the worst. To "apprehend with fear or regret" is something we've all experienced.

In this book I will concentrate on fear's effects and especially the last definition in my dad's dictionary, "to shrink from" or "be apprehensive about." I will prove to you addiction is your attempt to fight your fear with more fear and that all addiction is an addiction to fear.

Turning to confidence, it is an unmistakeable feeling of being when you have it. If you do not have confidence, chances are you would prefer not to talk about it.

Once again, according to the Gage Canadian Dictionary, confidence is "a firm trust; faith, as in self-reliance and a belief in one's own abilities. It is assurance or certainty."

In the pages ahead, I will convince you that the more fear in your life, the less confidence. Because that's how it works.

Part One, the first seven chapters I call the riddle, offers the information you need to resolve your addiction. In Part Two, seven chapters I call the twiddle (because it rhymes), twists and turns with supporting information. There are suggested readings for each chapter listed under Resources at the end of book's conclusion. Appendix A deals with reframing irrational beliefs. Appendix B contains twelve anecdotes in support of the book's contents.

Let us get something out of the way now and discuss false confidence. Liquid courage it is called.

I see it as a good sign when I've explained the fear seeker part of addiction and guys come back with the booze = confidence gambit. I'll explain more about fear seeking inside, but first let's meet Paul.

Paul is a guy who is shy as fuck. He will not talk to girls or ask them to dance or whatever else. He's gone online and, sure enough, he's self-diagnosed with "social anxiety disorder." He will say, "I have social anxiety disorder, man," labeling himself for credibility. This concerns our man, but he has found a way to solve his problem around people. He drinks when he's out. I have done the same, maybe you have too.

After a couple or three drinks, Paul comes alive and believes at times he is the life of the party—at least for a short while. From this he deduces he needs alcohol to survive social situations (because, after all, he has social anxiety ffs). I am in no way denigrating Paul's discomfort. You might empathize with Paul: as the pain of being left out is real, his desperation leads him to try anything to fit in.

Let me ask you: when do you run faster, when you are racing your brother or when a cop is chasing you? Not you? OK. How about if it is some big fucker about to pound you into the cement? Do you run faster then? How about when we read about some lady who lifted a car off her child after an accident?

We could say these circumstances exist on a scale of severity, with racing big brother close to the lower end and escaping a cop or the big fucker about to pound you higher up. Hysterical strength enough to lift a car off a loved one has to be tops, way at the higher end of our scale.

At the milder end, you find Paul using alcohol to get up enough nerve to talk to pretty girls and ask them to dance. He's not fighting for his life, but he's using the same basic mechanism, a super-mild form of "hysterical strength" to meet his challenge.

As with hysterical strength, or as with escaping from a bully, or as with reaching deep to face a fear or challenge, there is a kind of "I don't know how I did that" aspect to the experience. Paul feels the same way, remaining unsure of how he managed the social scene because booze fucks with his memory and learning, so he retains little that is useful later.

Not only that, in time, it takes him more and more booze to open up and relax. When two drinks do not do it anymore, he ups his ante. This leaves him a little confused. His focus is on a time it did seem to work, and he repeatedly tries to replicate those conditions.

In between drinking, Paul's social anxiety doesn't get better, it gets worse (I explain why beginning in chapter one, CRUX). So, in time, he drinks more, and more often, helpless as his confidence slides lower and lower. Booze becomes his only hope for social connection, something he desperately needs.

The very idea of not drinking is inconceivable because Paul believes he'd have to give up too much. He's sacrificing his tomorrows as wear-and-tear on his body and spirit continues.

He never realizes how he's piggy backing on his body's counter defense against the threat of dying from alcohol to go meet girls and dance. But just as hysterical strength doesn't last, neither does Paul's occasional alcohol-infused social prowess.

The most telling proof of this is he can't do it sober. He fails to develop a lasting concept for meeting and socializing with others that doesn't involve booze. This is the very definition of a failed strategy. The way forward for him is to be able to do it sober. If he does that, he wins.

Otherwise, he's bullshitting himself.

That's not the only falsehood around booze, drugs, and addictions I'll tell you about.

My favourite is when someone suffers under addiction, and the people around him say, "He's got to hit bottom before he can get better." It's as if that gives everyone a pass. Maybe it is true, maybe not.

I have a different point of view. It's what Tony the Restaurateur from Cornwall, Ontario, once told me decades ago. He said, "Chris, I believe anyone can be walked. It is just a question of approach."

I'm going to give you some of that in the pages ahead.

Christopher K. Wallace

PART ONE: THE RIDDLE

Riddle: a puzzling fact, thing, or person...

1. CRUX

In this chapter I'll discuss:

1. Crux Introduction

2. Crux Talk

3. Crux Bamboozle

Crux Introduction

I would like to explain what is at the crux of addiction. To make it easy and simple, I will tell you about it in a short dialogue, variations of which I have had dozens of times. If any of my current or previous clients read this, they are sure to remember when we had this conversation.

Some were addicted to alcohol, others to drugs, some to booze and drugs. The worst cases might have injected cocaine or methamphetamine and heroin, "speed balling" the two simultaneously. Plenty of men were cannabis addicts. Still others had what are referred to as process addictions, such as gambling, gaming, porn, sex, or even shopping. Some had a food habit that had them by the throat. I say throat because some also binged and purged their food daily. Many smoked cigarettes and vaped nicotine or cannabis derivatives.

Most but not all had seen a therapist, often including a marriage counsellor, and/or may have been in drug and alcohol treatment (a few of them more than once). I tend to see guys who are still employed because I must charge a fee to support people in these circumstances.

There are some good counsellors out there. It so happens I often counsel men who have seen therapists for years. Sometimes I advise men who are master's degree level therapists themselves, even the odd PhD psychologist, though, in those cases, rarely specifically about addiction. I also suspect that when a client is not paying for the service out of pocket, and the counsellor receives their payment from the state or an insurance company, the state or insurer is the true client. I fault no one for this; it is human nature.

While I have some experience helping men who were down and out, I cannot say what effect my ideas about how we approach addictions would measure up with the most vulnerable populations. I find that if a man does not have a place to live and a future to behold, he may lose his ability to defend himself.

That said, if a man is housed and fed and has at least the possibility of working, what I say here holds.

Crux Talk

For a general representative for addictions, including porn, drugs, binge eating, shopping, gambling, and gaming, as well as alcohol, we are going to have a talk with none other than Joe Six-Pack.

Joe is a guy who drinks most days, but not always. He can have periods of less drinking or none at all. Despite his beer habit, he still manages to hold it together (more or less). However, by the time Joe Six-Pack and I have our time together, there are widening cracks appearing at the seams of his life.

It may be a job loss, a promotion that did not come through, extra care required for someone in the family, a DUI, a deep unhappiness, a bad fight, a breakup, or a social catastrophe in the making. Just as often as not, there is some gal in the background putting pressure on Joe Six-Pack to get help.

Sipping Fear Pissing Confidence

The Talk...

Advisor to Men and Joe Six-Pack

These talks always proceed in a version of what follows:

"Joe, I know you are concerned about your drinking. Yet you are at least competent if not successful at your job, you live in relatively stable premises, you are the head of a family and all that entails, you keep vehicles on the road, you pay bills, and you have friends and family you still talk to and who still talk to you. So, what's up? What makes you think now is the time to look more carefully at this?"

Joe responds: "I do have all those things, and that's the thing. I feel the pressure. Usually I'll have deadlines to meet, management breathing down my neck, customers calling, and/or commitments to coworkers. At home, missus will have a list of things needing attention immediately or soon. I also need more time with my children, and then there is general upkeep and repair, finances, and taxes. It never ends."

"So, what do you do to manage?" I ask gently.

"I have a couple of beers to unwind, and sometimes I get a little shitfaced."

I look at him without saying a word and wait....

In a few moments, he goes further: "OK, let me tell you straight up, I often find myself drunk. This has the wife worried, and frankly I am a little concerned too. I guess I am feeling uncertain about my job, my

9

relationship, my children, my health, and my future. Truth is, I cannot seem to give it up."

"Joe, I hear you. Not being able to give it up is classic addiction, but as we talk more, you'll discover how that happens through no fault of your own. For now, what if I told you I don't think you are so much addicted to beer as you are addicted to fear."

"What do you mean?"

"Well, have you ever been afraid?"

"Sure, plenty of times."

"Think of those instances now, things like getting cut off on the highway during a rain or snowstorm; or having a close call with a big bully at the bar; or experiencing accidents or a calamity that rattled you and made you feel you had to run away or stand and deal with it no matter what. What your body and brain did in those circumstances was raise your heart rate and blood pressure and shallow your breathing so you could concentrate on the one thing that you needed to do to survive. Follow me?"

"Sure, fight or flight. I get it." Actually, he's unsure of where I'm headed.

"Fact is, Joe, at the crux of every addiction is a quest to narrow focus and relieve stress. That's what gives you relief. It's taking many thoughts and turning them into fewer thoughts or, at least, different thoughts. This allows you to get by and escape feeling overwhelmed."

"Interesting...," says Joe, eyeing me curiously, "... but what's that got to do with my drinking?"

"Fair question. Let's say you've had a tough week. By Friday you've had it up to here!" I gesture to about midway up my forehead. "Ever felt like that?"

Joe replies immediately with a chuckle, "Yeah, last week. In fact, most weeks, dammit."

"Exactly, and so you and your friend from work head to the bar late Friday afternoon to chill for a couple of hours before heading home once traffic dies down. You are about to leave one set of demands at work and head to another set at home. Follow me?"

"Yup, gotcha, welcome to my life."

"At the bar, you order a beer, down it, and then another. And by the second beer, you start to feel the buzz. What you don't realize is that at two beers your heart rate has gone up, as well as your blood pressure, and your breathing has shallowed. Now all you are thinking about is the game on the big screen and pizza." (Depending on Joe's age, I might say "pizza and pussy")

"That's true. I guess that is pretty much what happens."

"That's narrowing of focus. The booze has put you into a slight physiological fear state, though you don't experience it as such, and that has changed your thinking from many thoughts to different or fewer thoughts. That's what you were after. That's why you drink in the first place, to narrow focus."

"Holy shit. I've never looked at it that way."

I repeat, "You're not addicted to beer, Joe; you are addicted to fear."

Joe thinks about it for a minute. Then he says, "I am starting to see it. So, what does this mean?"

To which I reply, "There's more. Outside of severity, fear is fear in most circumstance, but addictions fear has far reaching effects, which I'll explain."

(Continued in chapter 2, read Crux Bamboozle first)

Crux Bamboozle

There is nothing in it for nature to make men and women the same. I want to say something to you, the reader, about women and alcohol. After getting off to a slow start, I drank on and off for more than forty years. Looking back, not one time can I say it added to my life.

Furthermore, in my view, neither did it bring much value to the gals I dated or with whom I had relationships. Alcohol often compromised the women around me and on occasion left them despoiled. Despoiled, I say….

The song by Eric Burdon and War, *Spill the Wine,* came out in 1970. All during my teen years, I never realized I twisted the song's meaning completely. I heard *"A little wine, get that girl,"* when the song said, *"Spill the wine, get that pearl."* It would not be the last set of lyrics I would butcher.

The song was about a time someone knocked over a bottle of wine at a jam session. I thought the catchy tune was a grape-incited celebration of women's carnality. It fit with "Candy is dandy, but liquor is quicker," something else I heard often from the older guys of my era.

I have seen women do things when drunk or stoned I am certain they would never do otherwise. I know too much now to ever go back to enabling or tolerating boozy broads.

In my first decade of adulthood, I had no opinion on women drinking without a man there to defend her, because the thought never crossed my mind. The stupid shit we all did while hammered was because "drunk men tell no lies." I carried so much shame, that I had low expectations of myself and others. Back then I was also naïve about women and alcohol. Now I blame women's lib. Ha!

I also never liked the club scene if it meant picking up drunk women, though plenty of my friends did. Instead, the odd time I would go out with the wives and girlfriends was as their escort when my rounder friends were chasing tail on the side. Otherwise, it was not my thing.

From the outset with missus, we talked about alcohol. She had seen what drinking does both to women and to men. Early on I told her how I felt about women drinking without their man present. She agreed and decided she would only drink with me (when I still drank) or when I knew she was in a safe environment, or else she would abstain completely.

She has checked in with me ever since to make sure I am OK with her having a glass, not for permission, but as a courtesy. Like I said, I do not drink anymore but have sure appreciated that about her over the last seventeen years.

Hang in here with me and let me explain why I am telling you this.

It might surprise you to know that it wasn't until the 1890s that chemist geeks were pulling extracts out of the adrenal glands. Adrenaline itself was discovered in 1900 and in 1901 was isolated from the adrenal glands of domesticated animals. It is one of a number of hormones in the body that also act as neurotransmitters in the brain.

Adrenaline in the brain is called epinephrine or norepinephrine, and along with dopamine make up the catecholamines. Catecholamines fire together and figure in sympathetic arousal during fight or flight. They are also part of your learning and desire mechanisms. The catecholamines, vasopressin, growth hormone, and cortisol (informally) are commonly referred to as stress hormones.

Under fight or flight, the hypothalamus-pituitary-adrenal axis (HPA) controls stress hormones, among other things sending blood to arm and leg muscles readying the body for action. Heart rate and blood pressure go up, pupils widen while eyes narrow, and critical thinking gets put on hold as the hippocampus responsible for explicit memory and learning goes offline. (Read that again if you like, perhaps keeping Paul from the introduction in mind).

Under fight or flight, you either stand up to the threat or get the hell out of Dodge. You might also look to your friends for backup. With all that said, we arrive at what I want to focus on.

While researching my first book (*Drinker's Riddle*, 2015), I found the work of Shelley Taylor at the University of California, Los Angeles. Her group observed that threatened or stressed animals affiliated with each other instead of attacking one another. We all do this, looking to others for reassurance when the heat is on. The effect she called "tend and befriend" is much greater in females than it is in males.

Let me repeat. Taylor's group realized that women under stress (stress = fear) use a "tend and befriend" strategy. Men can also use tend and befriend but are far more likely to use fight or flight when under threat. Many practitioners use the word "fawn" instead of or along with "tend and befriend."

Why is that so important? Well, if alcohol puts the body into a fear state, it is no wonder we men drink 10 beers and want to fight someone. Not so for women. You know it, and so do I.

Shelley Taylor points out that the way women evolved over time is that they cannot so easily fight like men are able to when attacked. A woman cannot grab her spear and shield and fuck off into the woods, not when she also usually has caregiving responsibilities. Try running away holding a child and with Grandma slung over your back, you will not get far. So, women adapted. (Hopefully, while a woman stalls, the men circle back and save the day).

Over time, with children and others to look after whom she won't leave behind, she learned to tend and befriend. If she has to, she will negotiate for her safety as well as the safety of those under her care. Female mammals have done this for so long it is now part of their nature.

I would argue further that this instinct exists on a continuum. Patty Hearst's case and Stockholm Syndrome, where captured align with captors, are at the extreme end. At the other end could be a woman in a bar drinking alcohol, especially in novel circumstances where strangers are present, more so if the strangers are men.

All addictions involve various fear/desire conditions. Spencer and Hutchinson's research published in 1999 (and other research since) made it clear that alcohol engages the HPA axis, which puts a drinker into a fear state and ages them more rapidly (more about this in later chapters).

There are six "F" variations (feed, fuck, freeze, fight, flight, fawn) factoring in every addiction. This is true even in behavioural addictions that do not involve psychoactive substances (such as porn, gambling, shopping, gaming, and even binge eating).

There is no safe amount of alcohol. Even one drink a day shrinks the brain (see Huberman below). Two drinks, and your physiological response is a mild fear state. A man can more or less negotiate this condition, especially if he has a secure attachment style. A woman? Not as much. And not in the same way. In my experience, most women use tend-and-befriend or fawn when tipsy.

That gal you are drinking with might seem like she is sweet on you, but what if she is simply trying her best to survive the fear state created by being poisoned with booze? Does that change things?

Over the last 11,000 years of the agricultural revolution, men discovered alcohol causes women to give it up—ass in the air like they just don't care—and they have been buying women drinks ever since.

It is an alcohol clusterfuck sex difference, a crux bamboozle.

Summaries

At the crux of all addictions is a quest to narrow focus and relieve stress.

All addictions use fear to fight fear, like using fire to fight fire.

You are not addicted to anything but fear.

Alcohol activates fear and so does every other addiction.

There is no safe amount of alcohol; even one drink per day shrinks your brain.

Women in fear may use tend-and-befriend or fawn behaviours to survive.

The more times your brain is in fear, the more it defaults to fear in the future.

2. CONFIDENCE

In this chapter I'll discuss:

1. Confidence Displacement

2. Learned helplessness

3. Building Confidence

Confidence Displacement

Joe Six-Pack and I are having the conversation I call "The Riddle." Together, we have established that Joe's alcohol consumption puts his body into a fear state and that this fear state narrows his focus, providing temporary relief from the stress of daily life.

I ask him, "Think: can you be confident and afraid at the same time?"

Like most others I have asked, Joe must think about this one. He must weigh his answer while considering what are two almost opposite feelings. He might scan his memory looking for an exception that would allow him to say that in certain circumstances it is possible.

Finally, he says, "No, I don't believe you can." He has answered the same way most people do.

We will talk more about what might constitute an exception and why it is not an exception in a moment. For now, Joe's answer allows me to add another part of "The Riddle." I check to make sure he knows what displacement is by asking him to imagine what happens when we add stones to a full bucket of water. He gets that it will cause the water to spill. The bucket can only hold so much.

"That's the thing," I say. "The more time you spend in a fear state, simple displacement means less time in a confident state. Even if you could entertain both feelings under some circumstances, for the most part the two feelings are incompatible."

"What's the implication then?"

"What this means for you is that the more time you spend in a physiological fear state, the less time you focus on building confidence. What I find is that with regular drinking, like with any addiction, including mood altering drugs and process addictions like porn, gambling, shopping, or overeating, as confidence is displaced it decreases. In time, the guy's confidence trends downward. Follow?"

"Holy shit. I hate to admit it, but I can see that." Here, Joe might tell me about something that recently gave him pause, when he felt fear in a way he had not before, or when he failed to rise to a challenge the way he knows he would have when he was not so addicted. His inaction is telling me something about what I call the action/sensory inputs confidence continuum. More on this later.

Learned Helplessness

I keep going and say, "In time, when a man chips away at his confidence by chasing fear in this way, he can dig himself into a hole. That is when confidence becomes scarce. Under some conditions it can become something called learned helplessness. Any idea what that is, Joe?"

He answers, "I could guess, but why don't you tell me." I take his subtle impatience as a good sign: the full weight of what I am telling him is dawning on him.

I tell him, "That is when a man gives up on confidence altogether. He tells no one and forms a secret belief that confidence happens "out there" to others and may no longer be possible for him."

"That's so fucked," Joe says, and goes quiet.

"It is, and I felt the same way when I realized this. How important is confidence to you?"

"Pretty important."

I do not want to lose my connection with Joe by being the bearer of bad news, but I also want him to see what is at stake. "Stick with me here, Joe. Think of a time when you had low confidence and another time when you had high confidence. What is the difference?"

Joe tells me, and we both laugh at how, this is the epitome of a stupid question to ask a male.

"Exactly." I continue. "In fact, confidence is our juice, isn't it? That circumstance where you lacked confidence was damn painful. Am I right?" I answer for him, nudging things along.

"Yeah, it totally sucked," says Joe.

"It sucks for everyone. That is how I know about it. Someone once described confidence as the stuff that takes thoughts and turns them into action. And that is the thing with low confidence: good ideas, dreams, aspirations, possibilities, are often sidetracked; they get put on hold or held back."

I have Joe's full attention and, hopefully, yours too.

Joe might be thinking about how he is going to keep drinking AND build his confidence. That would be normal. We males are adaptable if we are anything...

Building Confidence

So, I continue with my explanation. "Joe, let us talk a little bit more about confidence. If you remember times in your life where you had lots of it and think about it a bit, you might realize your confidence came from actions. One qualification I mentioned earlier about sensory inputs is that the brain responds first to actions and uses perception to evaluate things.

"No one hands us confidence; we build it with actions in two ways.

"The first way is when we do something we have never done, like a kid who goes on his first roller coaster ride. He is excited… but he is scared shitless too! But he forces himself to go through it. When he rolls in at the end and realizes he has lived through it, he is changed. He no longer sees it as impossible. He might come off the ride and say, "Again!" out of the sheer thrill of finding himself intact. One thing is for sure: he is not the same kid he was before; he is a new updated version of himself. Has anything like that happen to you?"

"Sure. I remember stuff like that, plenty of them," says Joe. He tells me a couple of times he rose to challenges and built his confidence. I get him to hang on to those moments for a bit.

You too might want to think about times where you took a risk, conquered fear, and built your confidence. They all counted towards who you became up to that point in your life.

I keep going. "The second pathway to confidence is to build ability over time until it adds up to a level of competence. It is like when you start sports or a tough school subject as a kid. From season to season or semester to semester you get better and better. You go from novice to apprentice and, if all goes well, reach some level of mastery compared to your peers and who you were before.

Joe says, "Oh I've heard of this, like ten thousand hours applied to something?"

"Exactly. It is the time it takes to achieve mastery though not necessarily ten thousand hours."

Whether you come by confidence slowly or quickly, we earn every bit of the confidence we build.

Confidence also tells a person, "If I did this, maybe I could also do that!" which is not only a critical survival skill, but it may also be your key to building a life of meaning and freedom.

"Joe, how is this landing for you? Can you relate to any of this?"

Joe speaks slowly, carefully. The contrast is beginning to dawn on him with some force. He is shifting.

Memories of hangovers, awkward social situations, disappointed loved ones, hidden talent, and lost chances at work or even when he risked his job, all these self-evident scenarios, flash through Joe's mind's eye and become clear.

We talk about some of these experiences, and as he remembers, his voice is lower, his words deliberate, but it is here I want to remove all doubt in support of my contention that fear is what drives his drinking.

"Joe, let's say a boxer is entering the ring to fight a big opponent. Leading up the fight, while training, he might bounce between confidence and fear, and hopefully he leaves all his fear in the gym. By the time he climbs into the ring, unquestionably, to survive he must feel invincible.

"Or what about that guy who set a surfing world record a few years back. You can imagine him on top of an 80-foot wave off Barcelona and telling himself, 'Oh shit!' and 'I got this!' and 'Oh shit!' and 'I've got this!' back and forth. Again, his training will carry him through. He has prepared for years for such a chance. He tells himself, 'This wave is mine,' 'I am one with the wave,' etc. It is next-level stuff.

"Or a paratrooper who is about to drop out of an airplane behind enemy lines. Damn straight he was scared the first time he practiced jumping. But he started that big jump a long time ago by first jumping off a two-foot-high box and then proceeding in small incremental steps, higher and higher, repeated a thousand times. When he is in theater the warrior in him takes over, and he moves with a confident execution automaticity built from hours and hours of rigorous practice in the toughest conditions.

"All three of these men have big challenges before them. They might have been able to vacillate between two opposing feelings in the face of contemplated risk but not now in the moment of execution.

"Our boxer might get knocked out, suffer brain damage, ruin his career, and wind up a vegetable. Our surfer could be crushed by tons of water and drown. Our paratrooper is jumping out of a fucking plane to possibly get fucking shot at and die, Joe!

"Years of preparation allow them to prevail. Those men must defend every ounce of confidence they come across and not allow anything to fuck with it, so they train hard.

"With drinking, as with any addiction, the fear state you create is absent visible threat.

"Think about that for a moment.

"There is no jump from a plane, no giant wave threatening to drown you, no big mother fucker about to try to bash your brains in. No. You are sitting down in a pub or at home on your couch or at your table with your heart pounding, breathing shallowed, and blood pressure up. But there is no threat.

"This confuses the fuck out of things…

"… without real danger the brain and body in a fear state cannot trust its own survival instincts. And that kills confidence. Amongst other ill-effects, like priming the body for fear, confidence is the first to go.

"So, ask yourself, Joe: how much fear do you need to sip on to piss out even more of your confidence?"

How much more gambling risk do I need to tolerate to sweat out more of my confidence?

How much cannabis do I need to inhale to exhale more of my confidence?

How much porn do I need to watch to ejaculate more of my confidence?

How much food do I need to stuff into my mouth to shit out more of my confidence?

"Ask yourself, Joe: How are you going to claim and rebuild your lost confidence?

"And there is more…"

Summaries

Confidence is the stuff that takes thoughts and turns them into actions.

You cannot be in fear and in confidence at the same time.

You can be in fear, or you can be in confidence, not both.

Confidence is won by taking bigger risks and by incremental improvement adding up to competence.

Confidence is earned through actions and maintained through practice.

When confidence is displaced long enough, learned helplessness sets in.

Actions beget confidence, which begets actions, which begets more confidence.

3. WANTING

In this chapter I'll discuss:

1. Wanting and Suffering

2. Wanting and Fear

3. Wanting-Suffering Cycle

Wanting and Suffering

Let me see if I can impress upon you one of the fundamental ways to deal with an annoying (or life-threatening) addiction. That is to be on the lookout for wanting. We must adopt the view that wanting signals a need for us to pause and consider things. You would not buy a significant number of stocks, or real estate, or even a new set of living room furniture on a whim. Not usually. Taking the time to consider things while imagining the future is one of our best attributes.

Arthur Schopenhauer (1788-1860) said, "All willing arises from want, therefore from deficiency, and therefore from suffering." He is saying that as soon as we want, we must contend with not getting, and this is painful to contemplate. In summary, wanting equals suffering. The Buddhists have known for more than two thousand years that desire and suffering go hand in hand.

Here is some super simplified layman's neuroscience. Electricity and specialized chemicals run the nervous system, which is comprised of neurons and their sidekick cells, the glia. It is estimated there are 86 billion neurons in the brain alone (give or take a few billion). WE also have millions and millions of neurons all over our body, including 100 million in the gut.

Neurons have a main body, and a tail-like part called an axon, some several. At the end of each axon is a synapse, which is a tiny space between two neurons. Neurons fire and release chemicals, which are then taken up by landing sites on the next neuron to continue a signal.

There are a few dozen neurotransmitters, and once discharged from neuron to neuron, these chemicals make their way back to their originating neuron in a process called re-uptake, there ready to be fired again. Neuromodulators are neurotransmitters that change how we feel, and they affect many parts of the brain.

A bunch of neurotransmitters you may have heard of make you feel good in the moment. These include endorphins (a natural pain killer), serotonin (a mood stabilizer), oxytocin (the love hormone), acetylcholine (calms you down) and anandamide and cannabinoid receptors (create bliss like cannabis does).

To aid in survival, however, we have less capacity to feel good than to feel bad.

The future-focused catecholamines dopamine and adrenaline, which function as both neurotransmitters and hormones (through their neuropeptides), activate survival mechanisms like "getting" and "freeze, fight, or flight." (Note: as mentioned, adrenaline in the brain is called epinephrine & norepinephrine but is the same thing). Feel-good dopamine and the stress hormone adrenaline are both present during learning and during fear.

It is these catecholamine survival neuromodulators that figure most in addiction. No kidding, you might say, having heard plenty about dopamine. The difference for me, though, was that in 2014 I realized dopamine and adrenaline operate together. Measured against my own addiction experiences, I realized a wanting or desire state is also a fear state… and this was costing me confidence.

Wanting and Fear

I can say an addicted man is seeking fear because wherever you find dopamine firing you also find adrenaline. Together, the activated catecholamines narrow focus and help deal with his stress using fear. The nervous system is trained by experience, so as he feeds wanting, he's growing suffering.

Wanting causes the catecholamine dopamine to fire at ten times normal. The brain adapts to how we live, so the second and third time we do something tends to bring less and less gratification.

Satisfaction in the present is by far the weaker of the two neuromodulating systems. To simplify: your "get" system is far more powerful than your "got" system.

When rewards disappoint (inevitable under habituation), dopamine firing stops entirely. You feel this kind of let down physically. That is another way in which wanting kills confidence.

The first time I ate lemon meringue pie as a kid I thought I'd died and gone to heaven. Now? Not so much.

I stay away from it completely except each year on New Year's Eve when I pick up two pies from Loughlin's Country Store. I give one to a friend who lives nearby and keep the other for missus and kids.

Despite tasting it only once a year, the thrill is gone, partly because I can never have my first piece of lemon meringue pie ever again. It just wears out. My nine-year-old son says it is by far his favourite pie. Chip off the old block, that boy.

How many things can you think of that once held your interest and then did not? Anything once obtained quickly loses its allure. An interesting aside is that a two-beer buzz does not get better with more beer. In fact, despite trying… it gets worse. You cannot recapture a two-beer buzz by drinking more beer.

If one piece of lemon meringue pie will not do it anymore, some will try two. Like the two-beer buzz, you cannot re-experience your first piece of lemon meringue pie by eating more of it. In short order and with no one watching, a guy might eat half a pie at a time, and eventually, a whole pie in two sittings within hours. Some day he buys a pie knowing he will eat it all. That kind of preoccupation with wanting is what causes habituation. Think of the various ways you might be repeating this…

Catecholamines are supposed to activate for short periods of time to get stuff or for learning or for freeze, fight, and flight. These critical contextual states of desire and action serve survival. When catecholamines are firing under addictions, learned brain concepts become uncertain, and so confidence also becomes uncertain. We will talk more about this further on.

Often a wanting state can leave a person feeling shitty and screwed over once the object of their desire/fear is met because of the difference between expectation and actual experience.

The vivid memory of my first lemon meringue pie as a kid stokes my desire, while the actual experience has gotten old and so is a comparative let down. That is how the brain works. Wanting is suffering.

Wanting Suffering Cycle

FOMO is real, and what is the first word in the acronym FOMO (Fear of Missing Out)? If you want something, you risk not getting. FOMO results in fear and… more displaced confidence.

Once upon a time long ago, I spent a decade (on and off) addicted to heroin (which I swore I would never do). I can tell you trying to secure dope when you have a habit is fear-based and narrows the fuck out of focus.

Be it the next card turned over at the blackjack table, the next beer, the next cannabis bong hit, the next porn video, the next hit of heroin, cocaine, meth, Adderall, or anti-anxiety meds, the next gaming level, or the next lemon meringue pie, searching for supply works to narrow focus… until it does not.

And that search is a confidence killer as you become enslaved to fear and desire.

When you feed the dopamine-adrenaline system, wanting does not decrease, it increases. This puts the brain in a perpetual deficit, displacing even more confidence.

Way back in time, I would have a joint after work to pull the curtain down on my day. Eventually, I added beer. Sure enough, two beers in I would want to smoke hashish. Over the years I built myself up to half a dozen beers and then switched to tall boys so I could keep it at six. I also learned how to make my own hashish, "Le hash qui assome" as a friend put it. That is French for Knockout Hash.

You see this with cigarettes for cocaine and meth users and/or beer drinkers too. Cigarettes can be smoked one after another. A guy is drinking or doing cocaine or meth and, as if that is not enough, still he craves more. So, he smokes, often almost chain-smoking. Nicotine kicks up the catecholamines and changes breathing, increases heart rate, blood pressure, and focus, and ramps up wanting.

More wanting creates more wanting… and that is suffering.

Think of it, nicotine does squat except create compulsive use. I have never met one person who told me the first time they had a cigarette they knew it was for them. To a person it was a bad experience. No one smokes and says, "I love the taste." Though, there may be some oddball out there who does.

There is no buzz with nicotine. People will get stressed at work and go out for a smoke to relax. I am not fooled; it is the increased heart rate and blood pressure narrowing their focus which displaces stress and gives that false impression. And when wired to nicotine they crave it to get rid of withdrawals, which makes them crave it more. It is the wanting-suffering cycle.

That people are addicted because they like it is mistaken and misses the point. It is fear they want otherwise there would be hardly any cigarette smokers.

Using catecholamines to delay dealing with your stress costs you precious confidence. Wanting is suffering, winning builds confidence; you must choose winning over wanting.

Otherwise, it is like you are fighting a real fire with more fire.

Stop doing that. It doesn't work. Eventually, it all burns to the ground.

Summaries

Where there is desire there is also fear; FOMO is real.

Wanting is suffering because you might not get.

Our getting drive is greater than our got satiation.

We have less capacity to feel good than to feel bad.

Wanting makes the brain create more wanting, and that is suffering.

Addiction is like fighting a house on fire with a flamethrower.

4. WINNING

In this chapter I'll discuss:

1. Free Will

2. Confronting Wanting

3. Defending Confidence

Free Will

Want to know why free will escapes you? Stop beating yourself up because you live automatically most of the time. In fact, we all do. You have a brain and brain stem, a spinal cord with peripheral nerves to your musculature, and two parts of the vagus nerve, the dorsal and ventral. This is your integrated nervous system. Trained by experience to keep you alive, it operates largely beneath awareness.

You can well imagine what an evolutionary advantage it is to have an adaptable system committed to running things without having to think about it. You learned to walk at age two and never thought about it again. It is like how a pilot on a trans-Atlantic flight uses autopilot. The captain flying the plane handles take off, landing, and emergencies. The rest of the time, he can talk with his co-pilot and passengers, even flirt with a stewardess, while the plane flies itself.

It works in a similar way in humans.

Like the plane's autopilot responding to conditions and experience (programming), your integrated nervous system will avoid anxiety and depression using denial, distortion, and even outright repression. Another name for your autopilot is the ego (Latin for "I," the default mode is related).

Every second, you take millions of bits of sensory information into the brain and body (the skin being your largest organ). Most times you are aware of fifty bits per second, a tiny portion of this massive data overwhelm. You can learn to control more of it, but it is not surprising people tend to let it run itself.

Whereas with a long-distance plane, autopilot must be purposely switched on and off, in the case of humans, the default setting is autopilot. All you get in the way of "free will" is an override... a "free won't" as one neuroscientist puts it. This means you better make good use of it.

Confronting Wanting

It is only with awareness that you bring about the possibility of change, something I will repeat often in this book. If a state requires thoughts, feelings, and focus, with even a little focus you can quickly learn to use your override system intelligently to confront wanting and start winning.

For survival reasons, emotions happen faster than we can think. After all, the brain evolved from motor activity in support of the body. I remember Mike Gazzaniga writing in *The Social Brain* that if we become aware of something, it has usually already happened. We interpret after-the-fact.

Keeping things simple, we retain a primitive response to fear through the basal ganglia to help encourage or inhibit movement, the amygdala-led limbic system to govern basic emotions, and the prefrontal cortex for executive function—where we decide if something is truly scary or not.

Each one has evolved from lowest to highest over top of the other. To replace wanting with winning, we concern ourselves with mesocortical over mesolimbic pathways, fancy words for thinking over feeling.

Lieberman and Long in their book *The Molecule of More,* and Anna Lembke in her excellent little book *Dopamine Nation,* refer to the mesolimbic system to explain how neurons from the dopamine-rich ventral tegmental area extend to an area in the midbrain called the nucleus accumbens and fire up desire. This creates wanting, fear of missing out (FOMO), and in Schopenhauer's view, "willing," and thus wanting and suffering. That it is "fear" of missing out tells us adrenaline is involved too.

Yet those catecholamine axons do not stop there. They continue to your mesocortical system at the prefrontal cortices, where focus allows you to shut off autopilot and take over the controls.

This is when you use your volitional override system to add a pause long enough to check your itch with an informal cost-benefit analysis, say Lieberman and Long. This is when you run the consequences of acting on a FOMO craving through your self-image and what you stand for.

On a recent podcast interview, Stanford professor Andrew Huberman explains what happens: when you put a pause in place to consider things, the left dorsolateral prefrontal cortex signals the vagus nerve to slow heart rate. This "gap," as it is called in the mindfulness community, gives you a break from anxiety (and craving) and instead allows curiosity and exploration. With a little practice you can learn to do this every time you are in a wanting state.

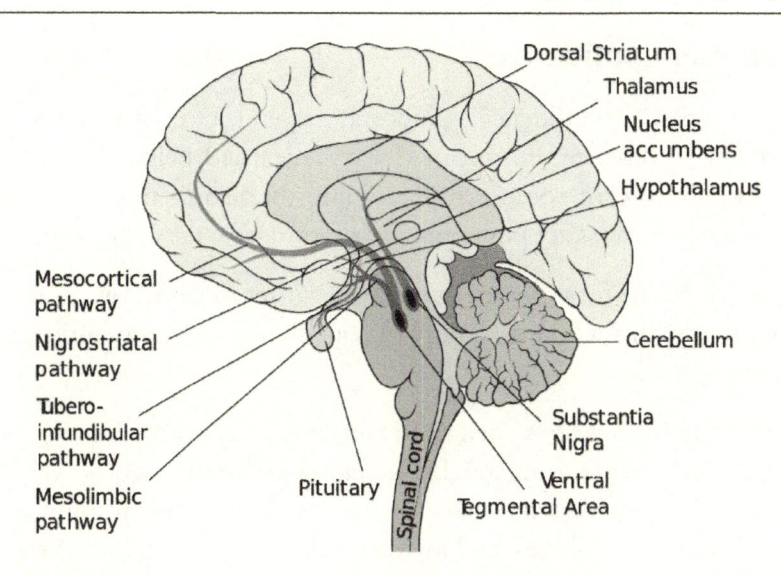

Figure labels: Dorsal Striatum, Thalamus, Nucleus accumbens, Hypothalamus, Cerebellum, Substantia Nigra, Ventral Tegmental Area, Pituitary, Spinal cord, Mesocortical pathway, Nigrostriatal pathway, Tubero-infundibular pathway, Mesolimbic pathway

* User: Slashme; Patrick J. Lynch; User: Fvasconcellos, CC BY-SA 4.0 <https://creativecommons.org/licenses/by-sa/4.0>,

Notice your wanting, and by using your power to purposefully focus, you will act above the automaticity of the nervous system; you will shortcut the co-opted survival process by shifting focus to your identity.

Listen to me carefully here as I explain why you must do this:

Unless you form an idea of who you want to be and decide to act on your own behalf, you will be put together by the vagaries of chance while meeting other people's needs instead of your own. That's classic Nice Guy Syndrome (also the title of a book you should read).

That is how it works. As a child you had no choice over this stuff. As an adult, you do. You were once the boy your caregivers made, but you can and will build the man of your future, for better or worse.

I can ask you to live up to your values and identity until the cows come home (as ma used to say), but if you have no idea of what matters to you, identity will be difficult to grasp.

Defending Confidence

Ask yourself why confidence is important to you. Even if you have not had much confidence, do not give way to learned helplessness. Fight back and act to earn some confidence and then some more. If it is of value, then you must act powerfully in support of your confidence.

You must go from someone who once suffered under wanting and replace that with a winning identity of your choosing. Pay attention: eyes wide open here.

You will still have desires such as the lust you have for the love of your life or an uncompromising need to defend your family and friends. You will still feel compelled to build your career, to serve your community, to love the sports, hobbies, and interests that serve your talents. You will still use your power and love in service of yourself and others to find meaning and freedom.

In each of these cases you will have paused to ensure your behaviour matches the man you claim to be. These prosocial wants have been considered, evaluated, and approved by your higher-order thinking.

Men defend, deliver, discern and define, discuss or delay to consult expertise or to sleep on things, and then decide. To me these are the seven action "D"s of masculine decorum. You must first defend…

When you feel wanting strike you in the body as cravings do, you take a stance and defend your confidence by declaring, "I'm not the kind of man who is ruled by wanting," and affirm your identity.

If need be, remind yourself "Wanting is for lesser men than me" and distance yourself from your former self. Reaffirm your claim on who you are now so as to defend your confidence even further.

And you may add in, "I am the type of man who wins instead of wants."

Or put more simply, "I don't want, I win." Or "Thank you, I'd rather win than want."

I dare you to sign your name to any of these bold statements. Make each of these a part of your repertoire of mantras to defend against wanting, so that you may continue to win at life. All it takes is a pause between stimulus and response, as Victor Frankl famously suggested.

You want to defend your confidence by discerning that wanting calls you. Here you can discuss it with yourself or someone with whom you have partnered in change. You delay acting to ensure you are making the best call possible. If you can see how every craving is an opportunity to confront wanting, you step into a more powerful existence.

It takes men a while to develop. The prefrontal cortices do not usually come fully online until his mid-twenties and some aspects into his thirties. It is no coincidence that many people who find themselves addicted quit on their own by age thirty, around when the steering wheel is fully installed.

At any age, use wanting as a signal to take over the steering controls. Declare a mantra aloud, if you must or can, to remind yourself of the man you intend to be. Look up one of the best poems for men, "Invictus," by William Ernest Henley, and read it every day. Do this now.

Confronting fear and desire are ways to grow confidence. Pain teaches, so make your suffering pay. Like lifting weights grows muscle, you find the uncomfortable emotions of fear and wanting are an opportunity to expand your being by refusing to take the path of least resistance to weakness.

Over the years, I have learned to catch myself when in the throes of wanting and to employ a countering strategy to lessen my suffering. Am I perfect at it? Not a chance. I am better, so much better than I was.

Meet desire head-on in daily life to build up mental muscle to inoculate yourself from desire's pain. Soon you will see FOMO for the dead-end it is.

I use my children in this regard. Each day one or both is asking me for something. If you came to my house, where I make them breakfast most mornings, and asked them "What is wanting?" one or both would tell you it is suffering. That one is easy.

What is harder for them is having to listen to me sing the Rolling Stones song, "You Can't Always Get What You Want" in my off-key baritone. Eyes roll, and whatever they wanted soon becomes frivolous in the face of dad's aversive conditioning.

If you asked them at that same breakfast table "What is happiness?" they would tell you it is a decision. As I teach them, to help with their disappointments in general, I also remind myself.

Like I said, I am not perfect at this wanting thing. Distracted, I will spot some gadget advertised on social media and, on a whim, buy it. I live on 200 acres of bush, and it is dark at night (of course). The best rechargeable flashlight I own I bought online, but two of the worst rechargeable flashlights I own are sitting on one of my bookshelves as I write this, also bought online.

Hitting a winner like my best flashlight does not fool me. I know exactly what I am doing when I engage in this kind of impulsive shopping. How do I know it is impulsive? I had no intention of buying a flashlight. I have flashlights, in fact, I even have electricity.

Yet, I bought them. I keep the two duds in sight on my bookshelf to remind me of how wanting is suffering. Token symbols to anyone else, I know their true value.

These are small potatoes compared to how I once was. In the early 1990s I ran large sales team in Southern Ontario and would visit malls while my reps were at work. Some days I would spend more than I made. I had items of clothing in my closet with the price tags on them for months, years even.

By then I had given up heroin and cocaine, so shopping seemed mild in comparison. Watch for this trap.

Men give up hard drugs or a bad booze habit, and they get the idea it is OK to still smoke cigarettes or vape nicotine or watch porn or "just game." Some might hit the gym to counter an addiction and make up for lost time, and wind up injured a few months later. Then, bored and restless, they risk relapse. Obsession is magnified desire and fear, and we need to check all desires to ensure we are still winning.

I am afraid it is not until we realize the myriad ways in which wanting creeps into our lives and adds to our suffering that we bring the possibility of less suffering.

It was not until I could appreciate how the catecholamines dopamine and adrenaline worked to erode confidence that I pieced together what was happening to me and to the men I worked with.

Like the Stones song declares, "You can't always get what you want, But if you try sometime, you'll find, You get what you need."

What you need is to decide to want less... and start winning more. I learned wanting is suffering... and a suffering man is not a confident man.

Summaries

Most of your brain is on autopilot.

You don't have free will; at best you have free won't.

You are aware of less than one tenth of one percent of the sensory inputs coming into your being.

Shit happens, and then you get the story created by your predictive brain.

Defeat wanting by kicking desire and fear upstairs to be evaluated by values and identity.

Wanting is for lesser men than you.

You are the type of man who wins, not the type of man who wants.

Confronting fear and desire grows confidence.

Wanting is suffering, and a suffering man is not a confident man.

7 Decorum Ds of Masculine Action

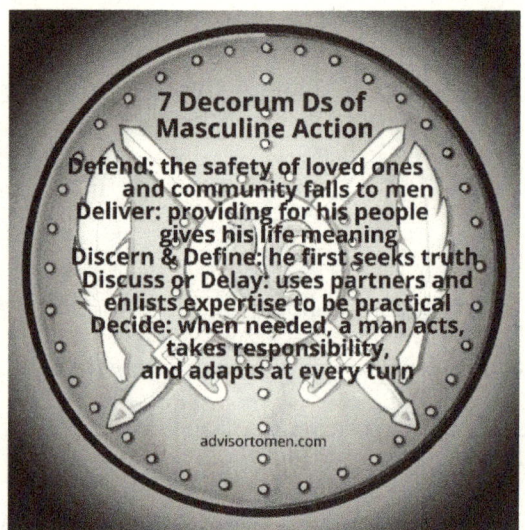

Defend: the safety of loved ones and community falls to men
Deliver: providing for his people gives his life meaning
Discern & Define: he first seeks truth
Discuss or Delay: uses partners and enlists expertise to be practical
Decide: when needed, a man acts, takes responsibility, and adapts at every turn

advisortomen.com

5. TESTING

In this chapter I'll discuss:

1. Relapse

2. Triggers and Consequences

3. Testing improves Abstinence

Relapse

When someone quits an addiction, enjoys a period of sobriety or abstention, and then goes back to active engagement in their addiction, the addiction pros call that a "relapse."

Why do people relapse? It happens because of how addiction is learned.

It is like riding a bike.

When you learn to ride a bike, there are seven or eight behaviours you must control: sitting, pedaling, balancing, braking, steering, watching your front wheel, being aware of your surroundings, listening for cars, etc. At first you fall over and struggle but soon enough, you get it.

A week later, you can ride by your house and say, "Look, Ma, no hands!" These seven or eight behaviours have become "chunked" into one thing, what we call "riding a bike." You do not think of each behaviour anymore; the whole sequence of riding a bike is one automatic thing.

Now, stay off a bike for a decade or two, do you ever forget how?

After learning to ride a bike, you can jump on a bicycle at any time in your life, and after a couple of wobbles, off you go. You never forget and ride it like always. Addiction is learned the same way.

From trigger to reward, the behaviour is "catecholamine chunked" near the brain stem and forebrain, the striatum (go, no-go circuit) and infralimbic cortex (habit formation) areas, so it becomes automatic.

The catecholamines adrenaline and dopamine are involved because adrenaline is always involved in new learning, and new learning is desire driven. Besides, it's scary learning how to ride a bike.

After a relapse, people will tell you that they did not even realize what they were doing, that they "suddenly" found themselves in a bar, putting glass to lips or walking out of a liquor store... or at the casino or racetrack or pulling out their credit card, ordering a big meal, searching for porn, or engaging in whatever addiction they have.

This is the compulsive aspect of addiction, an automaticity happening below the functioning thinking cortex. And, once you have learned it to this level, there is usually no going back.

What do I mean? Can you unlearn how to ride a bike?

Exactly. So… you've got to stay off the bike.

Triggers and Consequences

As you read this, remember that as long as you learn what I am teaching you. There is no going back.

Life's complexity demands daily adaptation. Rather than having to relearn the same thing repeatedly, the brain remembers an experience and adds it to a repertoire of "concepts" it uses in the future. Just as you learned to walk at around two years old, got good at it over the next year or so, now you do not ever have to think about it. Just like you learned to ride a bike.

Most of your learning happens the same way. The actions you engage in now train the brain for the future. Called neuroplasticity, the automaticity advantage bites us in the ass when it comes to addiction.

Let me give you a version of how this works. Behaviourists Ivan Pavlov and BF Skinner showed how all behaviour can be described by what comes before and what happens after a behaviour.

Pavlov focused on the before when he noticed his dogs would salivate when they could smell supper. He rang a bell at that precise moment and soon found that his dogs would salivate at the sound of the bell alone. Classical conditioning is when a stimulus (bell) and response (supper smell) become paired.

Skinner focused on the after when he showed how behaviour is maintained by the positive (adds something) and negative (stops something) consequences that follow a behaviour. If you are praised and encouraged for making your bed, you are likely to keep doing it; while the irritating sound of a ringing phone compels you to answer it. This is known as operant conditioning.

To simplify things, we can describe before and after cues and consequences of a behaviour as an ABC set, or antecedent-behaviour-consequence. In our case, it helps us see how something cues up addictive behaviour and is then sustained by consequences.

Consequences might be something added like the buzz you get while using mood altering drugs and alcohol or the fear/excitement and physical sensations of any process addiction, and/or something stopped when we narrow focus to lessen stress while in a mild physiological fear state.

Addictions are triggered by personal cues or triggers dependent on your experience, yet there are categories that show up repeatedly. Experiences allow the brain to create shortcuts as it applies a learned solution on autopilot.

To my way of thinking, addiction is repeatedly and negatively ceding control over your being to the body and circumstances using catecholamines in a quest to narrow focus and relieve stress. Do this often enough and a predictable relapse pattern develops as the thinking brain is co-opted by preceding learned triggers. Here is a list of some typical antecedents.

People: Misery loves company. Who do you need to stay away from or even cut out of your life?

Places: What are some places that are associated with your addiction?

Things: What things would you need to get rid of to stop being triggered by them?

Hunger: Low blood sugar can cause confusion and a search for calories in food, beer, etc.

Anger: How can you learn to manage underlying yearnings to feel less powerlessness?

Loneliness: Belonging is a top need, and how we regulate homeostasis reassuring each other.

Fatigue: Being tired means less will power as the body's needs take over thinking.

Boredom: Feeling bored can be so uncomfortable you prefer a compensating fear state (fear-seeking).

Restlessness: Dysregulation between energy, feelings and thinking often precipitates addiction.

Access: Easy access shortens the time between stimulus and response, thereby facilitating addiction.

Sickness: When the body and/or mind is ill, it may seek medicine to alleviate pain or discomfort.

Insomnia: Health and survival depend on sleep and so, difficulty sleeping is a common entranceway to addictions.

Success: Secret disbelief or entitlement in the self leads to "what if?" or "now what?" wanting.

That last one might surprise you, but when things are going well the feelings might be hard to manage, something you will learn more about later on in the book. The tendency to play small is real. For now, do any of these antecedent conditions start your addictive behaviour?

When you feel a craving, where do you feel it in the body? What thoughts come with it? What feelings? Get a sense of those feelings of urgency and discomfort or even excitement. If you can, write them down. Notice how these are learned responses you have taught yourself over time.

Now ask yourself what it gives you. What are the consequences that sustain your addiction? What does engaging in your addiction behaviour add? What does it take away? Jot these down somewhere.

In my first book, *Drinkers Riddle,* I referenced Roy Baumeister's book *Escaping the Self.* In it, he mentions the older executive who drinks a bottle of wine at night, arriving to work with a slight hangover each day. If he has a good day, he tells himself, "Not bad for a guy with a hangover." If he has a bad day, he tells himself, "No wonder, I was hungover." Consequences held in reserve.

Consider for a moment how your confidence is displaced while engaging in your addiction. The catecholamine combo of fear and desire experienced during craving and/or while engaging in addiction are incompatible with true confidence. You don't need to defend your confidence if you provide yourself an alibi like the executive in Roy's book. Note those consequences too.

Does an addiction build your faith in yourself, take some of it away, or keep it neutral? If you are honest, chances are you can see how your confidence suffers while distracted by the catecholamines, fear and desire. The confidence of an addicted man erodes in time.

Testing for Abstinence

When men first discover that it is fear and desire running them to narrow focus, they may feel compelled to evaluate it. Only now, instead of blindly engaging in addiction, they see clearly.

You can think about what triggered your addictive behaviour, taking a closer look at what happens just before. You can also figure out what consequences were derived from your addiction by examining the payoff. Finally, notice how these events are incompatible with confidence.

Leaving all judgment aside, you see how you have given up longer term gain to avoid short term pain engaging in your addiction. As with exercise or learning, you and I both know a better way is to endure short term pain for long term gain. The idea is to expand into life, not shrink from it.

I know, easier said. Yet, we must. There is no other way.

Identify which broad categories from the antecedents listed above best fits your circumstances. Is there one or many or do all fit in context? You may have specific circumstances that govern your addiction. What are they? The last time I drank I was aware, confirmed all that I knew was happening, and have never drunk again since. Been there, done that.

Testing an addiction is an occasion to switch off autopilot, take back the controls, and learn from the experience. Armed with this knowledge you can cut yourself some slack in the form of humility.

We all make the best decisions for ourselves at the time. That is always true. Only you can decide what is best for you using what you know, honouring your ability. The trick is to not use that as a rationalization to say fuck it and continue blindly. There is no going back.

If you were learning how to skeet shoot with your new shotgun in preparation for duck hunting season, you might hit high, you might hit low, you might hit side to side. Hell, you might miss the skeet completely at first. Would you ever stop aiming for the clay flying overhead? Make your aim true.

When a behaviour is no longer supported by antecedents and consequences its appeal tends to die off in a process called extinction. It can take years for a trigger to "extinguish" itself. Extinction might hold for minor triggers but not so much for entrenched behavioural sets (like riding a bike).

I can walk into an establishment, belly up to the bar, get a soda water and feel zero compunction to order an alcoholic beverage no matter what everyone else is ordering. Over the years I have chosen confidence over fear in so many situations in public restaurants and bars and elsewhere that they hold no purchase over my body and mind. That took time to extinguish helped by reinforcing an identity that precludes drinking, drugging, overeating, and any other addictions.

Yet, each trigger must be met head-on in isolation from other ABC sets (with some overlap).

For example, you might have resolutely overcome a tendency to eat and drink too much at Christmas dinner only to be blindsided by the following year's Thanksgiving get-together and end up stuffed and drunk when you had no intention of doing either. You beat Christmas but not Thanksgiving.

A man can quit drinking and find himself golfing with a couple of high school friends he has not connected with for some time. After an enjoyable round, at the 19th hole his buddies order a pitcher of beer. He tells himself he can manage raising a mug along with them. He thinks, "It's been five years, and look how well I am doing." Surely, it is no longer a problem. How many times do we find him months later drinking daily, right back to where he was (and drinking more from personal disappointment)?

A guy quits smoking and finds himself single. He meets a gal who likes a glass of wine and smokes when she drinks and, in the moment, he has a few drags on her cigarette. Later at the bar he buys a package of cigarettes. How often do we see him right back at his pack-a-day habit soon after?

You are an adult and so I will not tell you to quit your addiction. Realistically, most people need 90 days in which they "stay off the bike." Can't do 90? See if you can do 30 days and every month re-assess for 30 more. Many are happy with their improved quality of life and abstain indefinitely.

You could replace your addiction with something that feeds the spirit, a book, a hobby, or consider the categories body, spirit, people and work. Feed the spirit and find your zone. If you are physically capable, try Andy Frisella's "75 Hard." Watch for obsession to the point of breaking though. You can always repeat it later so dial back notions of invincibility and focus on building confidence.

Others assess things at some point and attempt to "learn from their mistake." That was no mistake. It was a test. Let go of disappointment quickly and chalk it up to experience.

The trick is to have the humility to see how you have ceded control of your being to the body and circumstances in that moment of relapse to play at stress relief, rather than building lasting resilience while living according to your values and identity.

Don't overlook the reasons why you are choosing confidence over fear. Make sure you have considered how you intend to defend your confidence, the more reasons the better. See yourself at a critical juncture with only one way to proceed: away from fear and towards confidence.

So, what will you do?

Summaries

Addiction is learned the same way you learn to ride a bike: you can't unlearn riding a bike.

Success creates more addiction relapses than failure.

People, places, things, hunger, anger, loneliness, fatigue, boredom, restlessness, access, sickness, and success.

Addiction gives you a temporary out on the problems of life; this confuses the brain for next time.

That's not a relapse, it was a test. What did you learn?

It can take five years to extinguish a trigger, and some you never forget (like riding a bike).

Sipping Fear Pissing Confidence

This is just a suggestion…

BANISHING BOOZE

Don't drink, ever. It weakens a man. No problem gets better with booze; there is no safe amount. Being powerful and drunk are incompatible: There is no powerful drunk. You can be drunk or you can be powerful, not both.
So… choose one.

advisortomen.com

6. CAGING

In this chapter I'll discuss:

1. Body Thoughts

2. Caging the Wolf

3. Claiming Identity

Body Thoughts

They say we have 40 to 80K thoughts per day. Who knows? Even considering a low-end estimate of only 6K thoughts, which is a heck of a lot of thoughts, where are all of these thoughts coming from?

While at first it might seem difficult to separate the two (I'll show you how), when it comes to addictions it is helpful to see most of these thoughts as reflections from your body with some interspersed focused, brain-interpreted ideation originating from the real you. I know, that's a mouthful. Bear with me, it gets simpler.

Your body talks to you, and every once in a while you answer. Put another way, you are run by your nervous system, and conscious awareness is along for the ride.

An example is coming home and becoming impatient with a roommate. Later, as you sit wolfing down supper, you may have realized you had not eaten since much earlier that day. You said to yourself, "No wonder I was a little snippy. I was starving." You had become hangry. Grrr…

Your low blood sugar skyrocketed the hunger hormone ghrelin until it took over and got your full attention. Your hunger may have been made worse if you were also a little dehydrated. In that instance, the body controlled your thinking. Hunger and thirst change thinking.

If you are up late trying to get some work done, composing a letter, learning a new digital platform, studying for an exam, or doing any number of brain-taxing things, you may notice that your brain starts to let you down as concentration and willpower wane. As darkness falls, melatonin rises, while the will often says yes but the body says no.

Something as simple as watching a flick on TV and falling asleep is similar. Missus will agree to watch a movie with me and the kids and say, "I'll try to stay up." More than once, I myself have woken up after a show ended and wondered what had happened.

Let us say you are in an important meeting that is dragging on, and you need to take a piss. Your focus on the people talking around the table will take a back seat to the demands of your bladder: your answers to their questions will become short and swift. And if you suspect you need to fully evacuate your bowels, you will want to get out of there as soon as you can. Speaking of which…

A joke that has been around forever debates which part of the body is the boss. Various body parts each make their case, and none agree. The asshole closes up and mayhem ensues. The heart, lungs, brain, kidneys, liver, skin, and the rest of the body parts all become immobilized under constipation's "hold" and come around, forced to acknowledge the asshole's supremacy. The contention is this is why you do not need brains to be a boss, just the ability to be an asshole. Ouch!

What about when you have seasonal allergies acting up? Your eyes are a bit watery, nose stuffed, you sneeze often, and thinking is off. If you take an antihistamine, those have effects too.

Or when you start coming down with something as simple as a common cold. Men tend to feel those worse than the other sex; the "man-cold" is real. You might find your thinking subverted by your body despite best intentions.

Realizing how much the body controls thinking might make you sympathetic to menstruating women. Missus cops to it. "I'm starting my period," she will exclaim... and we both know that anything she says that day may not be the real her.

With that last one, I know you get it... and I could rest my case. The body communicates with the brain through a process called interoception, which includes where the body is in the environment (proprioception) and a sense of what is around you (exteroception).

Throughout evolution, as humans acted to expand their geography, diet, and repertoire of behaviours, the brain responded in kind. In *The Brain from Inside Out,* György Buzsáki, MD, PhD., writes, "The goal of the brain is to explore the world and register the consequences of successful exploratory actions to improve the efficacy of future actions. Thus, an action–perception loop learns to make sense of sensory inputs. Perception is what we do."

You can see how the brain forms from motor movement up in your own life: as you began to move around as a toddler, rarely before, your brain recorded your first memories. Immediately, your preconfigured brain organized these actions into remembered concepts. The brain uses these to make sense of your world and apply in the days ahead. This is a lifelong process.

The brain exists to support the body, not the other way around.

The vagus, the body's longest nerve, which winds throughout your torso from face to testicles, including organs, skin, and digestive tract, provides an example of how this works. Around 80% of vagus nerve neurons point towards the brain. This means there is four times as much signaling from the body to the brain as from the brain to the body.

Another example is the way your spinal cord acts instantly under threat and activates musculature all over the body. Triggered situational awareness is lighting fast. It beats by far your much slower thinking, which has to catch up to the body.

Last night I was locking up the back porch in the dark and thought about a time a racoon killed a new rooster. When I opened the door to the porch, the reflection in the door window from the kitchen light behind me also moved. Momentarily, I thought there was something down ahead of me as I looked through the window to the floor of the porch outside... something moving.

My whole body seized up in freeze mode, and I could feel my heart pound, my eyes narrow in focus, my muscles tense in readiness. I saw what really happened a moment later and calmed down, laughing. The body rules...

Clinician Deb Dana, in her book *Polyvagal Exercises for Comfort and Safety*, describes the vagus nerve in two parts: the lower dorsal vagus is an evolutionary relic from five hundred million years ago, whereas the higher up ventral vagus came about with mammals around two hundred million years ago.

We find the dorsal vagus in humans at the bottom, operating below the diaphragm, where it influences feeding, mating, and the freeze response. Next up is the peripheral system, which governs muscles, and the fight or flight response, which came about somewhere between dorsal and ventral vagus development. From chapter one, Crux Bamboozle, I have added in "fawn" which I guess to be between fight/flight and ventral activation.

The ventral vagus influences above the diaphragm—heart, lungs, throat, voice, and trifacial nerves—as part of your social engagement system. According to Deb Dana, when we turn to each other looking for reassurance we regulate emotional homeostasis.

In sum, most thoughts are interpretations by the brain arising from messaging coming from the body; various addictions are about ceding control over your being to the body and circumstances in a quest to narrow focus and lessen stress.

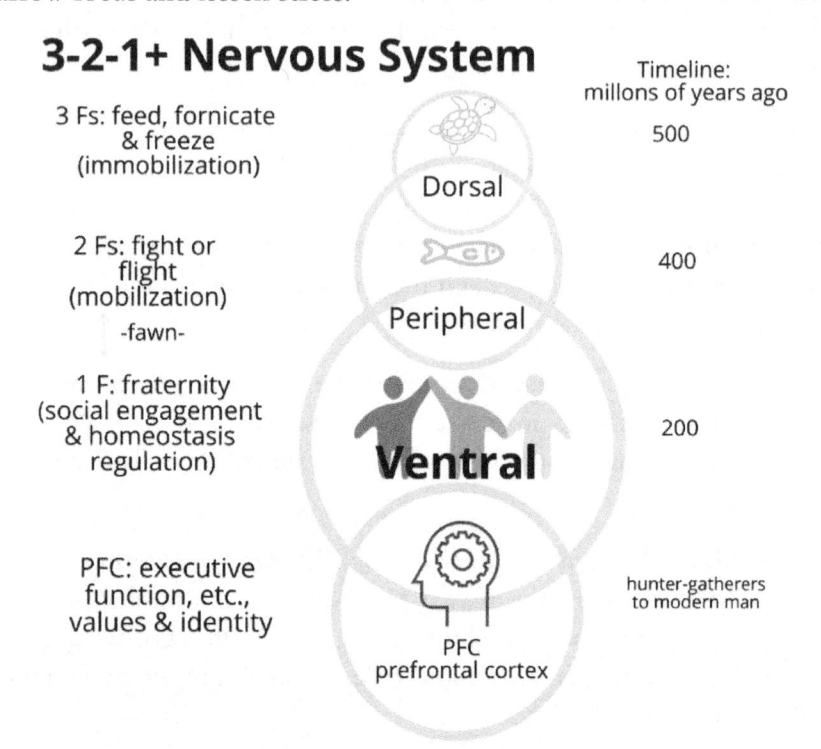

3-2-1+ Nervous System

3 Fs: feed, fornicate & freeze (immobilization) — Dorsal — Timeline: millions of years ago — 500

2 Fs: fight or flight (mobilization) -fawn- — Peripheral — 400

1 F: fraternity (social engagement & homeostasis regulation) — Ventral — 200

PFC: executive function, etc., values & identity — PFC prefrontal cortex — hunter-gatherers to modern man

*dorsal vagus, peripheral embedded in ventral & shaped by experience Deb Dana, 2022
**integrated nervous system denies, distorts, & represses inner and/or outer reality to lessen anxiety and depression George Vaillant, 1993

advisortomen.com

Ceding control of your being to the body is fine when jumping out the way of an oncoming car while walking across a busy street or having to deal with an annoying racoon infiltrating your back porch.

But a lot of the time, feeling stress and giving in to thoughts and impulses emanating from the body and then seeking escape through addiction instead of your more adaptive higher thinking is blindly allowing your lower order nervous system to rule you.

Caging the Wolf

You can fix that right now. Remember: with awareness there is the possibility of change.

It is a good idea to name this lower part of the self that tries to take charge, often despite wishes to the contrary. If you have tested your addiction, now is the time to call it out. Here is how:

The dorsal vagus and peripheral nervous system are of course extremely sensitive to stress, another word for fear. And remember fear and desire are close cousins. It just so happens The Wolf was one of the names I was called decades ago when I was a punk out on the streets. So, I call that lower part of me "the wolf."

The fear-seeking wolf gives zero fucks and is only about feed-fuck-kill-run-hide.

Glenn Livingston of *Never Binge Again* says not to confuse this part of you with your inner child, for there is no possibility of love from the lower order nervous system he calls the squealing pig.

Other men I work with have named this part of them the fucking ape, the chattering chimp, the slithering lizard, the hissing Gila monster, etc. An overeater with an online shopping habit named his lower nervous system Hippo while imagining how food and packages are devoured in its giant maw.

I call my lower self the growling, howling, whimpering wolf, but you might name yours something else.

Some call it "my addiction." I am fine with that as long as you do not label yourself into impotence. You do not have a disease. You do not have a condition over which you are powerless. You have automatic thoughts from the body like anyone else, and with a little knowledge you can learn to respond to them differently.

It is about the ascending Fs: feed, fuck, and freeze of dorsal vagus nerve; fight and flight of the peripheral nervous system (fawn strikes me as peripheral and semi-ventral); then to fraternity and friendship of the ventral vagus nerve social-engagement system; and of course, executive function, and values and identity of the prefrontal cortex up top. You must better understand your nervous system.

Instead of using the higher order ventral nervous system to connect with others and restore emotional balance while seeking a true expression of your talents, addiction uses dorsal vagus nervous-system immobilization and/or the lower order peripheral fight or flight to engage in protection instead of connection.

In protection mode, confidence is displaced. How could it not be?

The wolf can be cunning by providing thoughts from the body that hint at social engagement.

For example, by arranging to meet a drinking buddy or to be at a busy bar full of people; or to share the bong with someone or visit a dealer; or to encounter unknown faces and voices on the screen with cam girls, porn, or peelers at the strip club; or to gamble among others at the casino or game with players online; or to interact with shopping clerks, fawning over you and your credit cards at the mall; or to see overeating as a way to use delivery persons and eating as communal sharing of food even when bingeing alone.

Claiming Identity

How do you cage the wolf? First claim an identity.

How do you see your ideal self, and what matters most to you? If you were to live your best life, what view of yourself would that require? Do not fall for the "eyes see out" bullshit, meaning you need to fix "out there." Instead, claim an internal best self. Happiness is a decision, an inside job. You need to claim an identity for contrast and to live a life you can be satisfied with living.

The rule: Any thought contrary to your values and identity is the wolf. Better know what those are. Create clear rules for yourself around them.

Those contrary thoughts are not the real authentic you; they are lower-order survival impulses… so get good at calling out and caging the wolf's feed-fuck-kill-run-hide thinking. Live up to an identity of your choosing.

Your nervous system learns by trial and error, which means it can be reprogrammed. If you want new feelings, live new experiences. Take new actions to displace old habits.

If addiction is a "monkey on your back," you might say, "Thanks. The monkey wants to be addicted with me; however, I am not a monkey. I will pass." The ability to assert higher self builds confidence.

To arrive at being able to observe the monkey or wolf or whatever you would like to call it, move focus away from the body to the prefrontal cortex and your higher-order thinking. You must be able to shut off your default autopilot and take over the controls like a pilot does when encountering turbulence at 35,000 feet. Quoting Henley, "You are the captain of your soul." Did you read "Invictus"? Go read it now…

By using your override powers in these moments, you will notice what triggered your body, realizing what comfort/discomfort consequences the wolf was seeking. You will know how following circumstances and the body would compromise your confidence by giving into fear and a lesser self.

Once you realize how much you have ceded agency to the body, your life will change as you wrest control from the wolf and cage the beast. Demand that *you* run things. Use the rule.

Pissed off at someone? Holding a resentment? Plotting revenge? Rehearsing scenarios about telling someone off? Worried about tomorrow's meeting? These are all protection-based body thoughts. These are not the real you. Thoughts in those instances are physiologically based, and with one deep breath you can stop long enough to cage the wolf, refute the feed-fuck-kill-run-hide lower order thinking, and re-aim and reclaim higher identity instead.

Here's one more thing: what happens when you own a dog and refuse to train it?

The dog shits all over your floors, eats your furniture, books, doors, and pisses up against your walls. If it can reach your table or counter it will pull your meal down and eat it. An untrained dog will bite your guests, and when you intervene it might bite you.

Would you let that happen? Or would you train the damn dog but good. So, you know what to do.

Remember: wanting is suffering. You must replace wanting with winning. Say, "I'm not the type of man to be ruled by my body and circumstances; I am a man who lives according to his values."

You must claim an identity of your own or face dire consequences. Here is an 8-line poem shield in summary to help you think about this critical facet of your existence. I offer it here as a warning.

Cage the fear-seeking wolf and train the dog to build confidence in support of your identity.

Humans have trained wolves into domestic dogs over millions of years.

Eventually, descendants of the wolf became man's best friend.

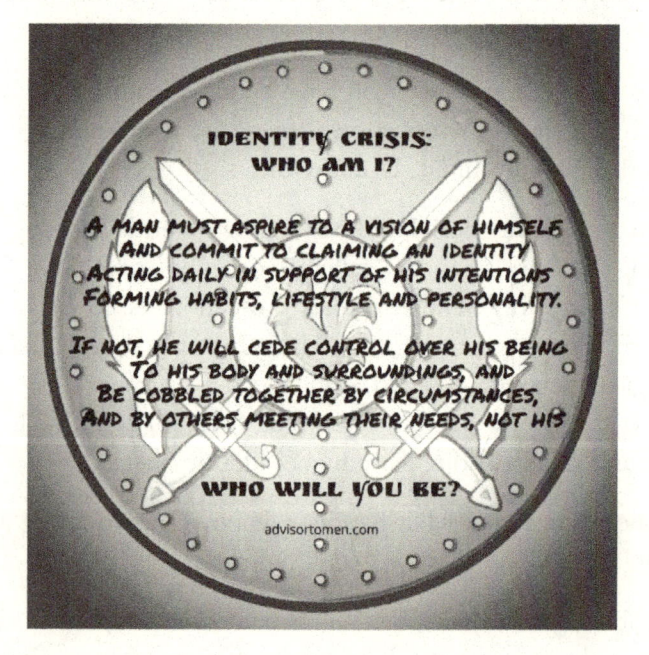

> **IDENTITY CRISIS: WHO AM I?**
>
> A MAN MUST ASPIRE TO A VISION OF HIMSELF AND COMMIT TO CLAIMING AN IDENTITY ACTING DAILY IN SUPPORT OF HIS INTENTIONS FORMING HABITS, LIFESTYLE AND PERSONALITY.
>
> IF NOT, HE WILL CEDE CONTROL OVER HIS BEING TO HIS BODY AND SURROUNDINGS, AND BE COBBLED TOGETHER BY CIRCUMSTANCES, AND BY OTHERS MEETING THEIR NEEDS, NOT HIS
>
> **WHO WILL YOU BE?**
>
> advisortomen.com

advisor to men trains his dog...

Summaries

Most of your thoughts come from the body, some even from your arse.

Being hangry is a perfect example of how the body takes over thinking.

When you are wired for protection over connection, your connections suffer.

Any thought that does not fit your values and identity comes from the wolf.

You wouldn't have an untrained dog in your home. Why have one in your body?

7. CHOSEN

In this chapter I'll discuss:

1. Chosen

2. Soul and Spirit

3. Purpose

Chosen

I want you to consider how you came about. Few people ever think about this, and it is worthwhile that we do. Let me start at the beginning...

Let us imagine it is likely you began as a gleam in your parent's eyes. We will skip ahead from there and go straight to the biological minutiae of their encounter. On the day you were conceived, there may have been more than a billion sperm vying for the egg (before plastics dropped sperm counts).

That is a billion possibilities. You could have been born a girl, a boy, and/or with any of a number of conditions. That you were conceived at all, and survived pregnancy and birth, is miraculous.

Reading this is a continuation of that miracle, the miracle of life itself, which we call a miracle only because of its mystery. As my mother told me on her deathbed, "Christopher, you have to have a little faith," and so I promised her I would leave a little room in my life for mystery.

You will say about being born, "It was the luck of the draw." I would like you to see it differently.

Using terms like "accident of birth" are ways we humans try to simplify things we do not understand. And when we do not understand something, we tend to make something up to make it familiar so that it feels less uncertain. To me, "accident of birth" is apologizing for being here, which you should not do.

Calling your birth and life an accident also means you believe you are bigger than nature. It is a stance which requires an incredible leap to the intelligence of an all-knowing being.

I say it is a mistake to say your life is an accident, or luck. You are not like someone who goes to Las Vegas and pulls the arm of a slot machine and waits for matched symbols to come up according to a predetermined calculation programmed into the machine. Nonsense.

Remember, unpredictability, uncertainty, and uncontrollability cause fear. It might seem like your existence was chance, like you won the "lottery of life" and, again, this is how we humans rationalise things. Fact is, you do not get to second-guess life itself in any way.

You might as well say the blue sky ought to be a lovely shade of yellow to match the sun. Or that green trees would look better if they were violet, chlorophyll be damned. Or that clear mountain streams should run black to match what could be falling black snow accumulating in hardened black glaciers high up on black mountain peaks (to contrast against a yellow sky). All ridiculous.

Calling your life and existence "luck" comes from a hubris or overreach borne from fear. The truth is the universe does not make mistakes; it just is. Nature is perfect. That you are here means you were chosen for life because nature deemed that your potentials and possibilities fit into her grand plan.

It behooves each one of us to appreciate these facts, to leave a little room for mystery as we accept nature's challenge to find ways to contribute.

Some of you will open your mind to this inner essence and be comforted and guided by it, while others are more content sticking to the biology. Either way, to live successfully means honouring your lifeforce on whatever terms and by whatever understanding works. It has to work for you.

Soul and Spirit

For example, epigenetic (environmental) influences on DNA are passed down through methyl groups for several generations. Methylation is what activates your chromosomes.

We know some kids ride well in cars, some sleep well, some eat well. Some do not. You can have an anxious child or a calm child, a curious child or a child who is relaxed. The list goes on. When you ask parents of several kids what is the same about their children, they will start to tell you what is different. You arrive here with a constitution which is all your own.

Our understanding of emotions has been updated to see them as predictive messages between body and mind (interoception) filtered through your databank of prior experiences (more on this later). Gyorgy Buzsaki argues we are governed not by a perception-to-action loop, but an action-to-perception circuitry and a brain preconfigured for action. We *do* perception, he says.

Carl Jung, Joseph Campbell, and many others have written about humanity's collective unconscious, evident in similar mythological symbols showing up over thousands of years in separate cultures on different continents. The Hero's Journey is at the root of every story of good over evil, triumph over challenge, and applies across mankind. We will talk more about Hero's Journey later.

For the sake of brevity, we call all these things various aspects of your soul. You may have thought about soul and spirit but perhaps not. Most people have an idea there is more to them than their daily performance, something which hints at their essential nature.

That the soul exists at all only needs that you sense it is there; moreover, the spirit is its voice. We could say one is past, one is future; one is static, the other moving.

For the sake of explanation, to feel the yearnings of the soul is to honour your lifeforce. It is where you go for grounding and certainty. It is everything in you and behind you.

Whereas the spirit is moved by life in the present, lifted by watching a sunrise, marveling the stars, walking in nature, appreciating each other, it is also what propels a man forward. He will say, "I felt my spirit calling me." Often it is just a stirring, a quiet whisper; nevertheless, it invites action, direction.

It is this spirit that fundamentally links you to your authentic self, that with which you were born and was subjugated as a child in conformity so as to not be abandoned by those upon whom you depended for survival. Later, you adopt persona, various masks worn at work, at home, at play, with different groups. These roles obfuscate the spirit even further.

But yet, if you slow and listen, the spirit manifests itself, often intuitively after a night's sleep, a walk, a shower, or out of nowhere. It may be part of a blessing, call it a benediction from the universe, by the same force behind the sun and stars that gives each of us life. Carbon = stardust. The implication is that your lifeforce is demanding that you manifest a powerful existence. That is nature's way.

Spirit is what connects you to awe, a sense that straddles excitement and fear as you consider forces greater than yourself. We often feel awe looking at a mountain or the vastness of an ocean, at great architecture and cities. The first time far from city lights and seeing the Milky Way you may have felt an overwhelming awe. The Northern Lights do that to me. But you can learn to see awe all over.

Because it feeds the spirit, awe opens your heart and mind to creativity, to potentials and possibilities. It is these two forces, the incorruptibility of soul and spirit, that anchor and guide you in your purpose.

Purpose

We hear and read a lot about purpose these days. "Find a job you like, and you'll never work a day in your life," goes the promise. To be sure, purpose is good, in fact it's essential for men to have a mission of some kind to follow. Most people overcomplicate things by searching for purpose, a frustrating approach. You can spend many years waiting for the right conditions for purpose to appear. It rarely works that way, and, of course, the risk is that you'll never find it.

It is much better to work your way into your purpose and let it find you. Here are some clues:

Viktor Frankl in his book *Man's Search for Meaning* taught that meaning comes from deeds, relationships, and overcoming obstacles. To be sure, there is a lot that can be filed under these broad categories. Raising children, creating a relationship that endures, producing something worthwhile, and doing good for each other while honouring our gifts are some of the ways.

Steve Chandler suggests you can shorten this into "making a difference." When all you need to do is to somehow make a positive difference each day, a great funnel of possibility becomes accessible.

Chosen for life by heavens of infinite wisdom, your purpose is to make a difference manifesting your talents nearby, expanding meaning and freedom to find your place in the sun.

You start with potential and possibilities, and these are hinted at by talents. Remember, the nervous system and brain are trained by experience. Talent plus intention create strengths, says Gallup. Life is short, so play to your strengths.

Each day, start with you, then move to the person next to you, and branch out from there. Ask "How can I make a positive difference?" Do that… Start small and grow accordingly.

To discover your talents, the Gallup organisation says to look for things you may have yearned for, perhaps during those times when you saw others doing something and you said to yourself, "I'd like to try that." Tony Robbins likes to say success in life is related to how much uncertainty you can tolerate. If you want new feelings, do new things. It might be cliché, but you either expand or die. Carl Jung said comfort zones are places where dreams go to die. Ouch.

When you lose track of time while doing something (sober), talent is often present. Similarly, surprise at how well you learn something new might also signal talent. Notice those activities you find satisfying and use them to hone your talents. Satisfaction is another sign talents are involved.

As if taking stone to steel, work your talents at something you find gratifying until innate talents sharpen and become your strengths. Use these to expand meaning and freedom. My psychology teacher Anita Roy (bless her heart) taught me the idea is to find your place in the sun.

By doing so you find a measure of freedom from the tyranny of this existence. In a four and a half billion-year-old planetary system, you will live within a single century. The only way I know to mitigate the suffering of this life is to do my best to make it meaningful. I repeat this, and not for the last time:

A man who uses his power and love in service of himself and others finds meaning and freedom.

When you are doing something you like that holds your full attention and comes with an increasing complexity (chess, not checkers), and during which emotions are temporarily suspended, you may find you lose track of time.

Mihaly Csikszentmihalyi (1934-2021 and pronounced chick-sent-me-hai) studied this phenomena in creative people and became known in the positive psychology movement as the "Father of Flow."

I suggest that operating in a flow state is when you are at your most powerful. Afterall, what could be more powerful than to feel like you stopped time?

The flow state is also called the zone. I contend flow is behind your craving.

The problem is you interpret the signals as fear and seek to escape using your addiction.

What if your cravings are really messages from the spirit demanding your most powerful self?

Sure, those feelings are uncomfortable in order to get your attention. Think about when you enter into your zone, those very emotions are then neutralized while your gifts (talents) are manifested.

You need more zone.

Every craving you have ever had was a calling from your lifeforce to engage in your zone of competence, to combine talent with intention and develop them into strengths.

You may realize now how with your addiction you have been running from the best part of yourself.

What if you re-read this daily until every craving compels you to act in the interests of nature, and you use your time to instead "take stone to steel" and build your strengths? Would that make a difference?

Otherwise, like many others, you may find that ten or twenty years go by. And one day you get lucky and run into someone like me who has made the same mistake.

And I will help you realize that you did not in fact live those ten or twenty years, but rather experienced a version of one year… ten or twenty times.

I myself realized this was a crime under the blue skies. It was a failure of the pact we all have with the heavens. Who would you need to be to be…

… to accept that you are a chosen one.

Summaries

You were chosen for life by heavens of infinite wisdom.

Second guessing nature is dumb. Nature is perfect. The universe doesn't make mistakes.

Every craving is a calling from your spirit demanding you live your most powerful self.

Creating a life of meaning gives you freedom from the tyranny of this existence.

You want to live ten years, not a version of one year ten times.

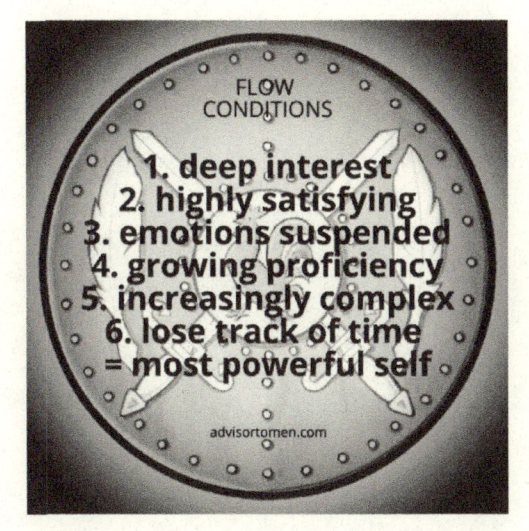

FLOW CONDITIONS
1. deep interest
2. highly satisfying
3. emotions suspended
4. growing proficiency
5. increasingly complex
6. lose track of time
= most powerful self

advisortomen.com

PART TWO: THE TWIDDLE

Twiddle: a series of small twists and turns...

8. TRAUMA

In this chapter I'll discuss:

1. Guilt

2. Shame

3. Trauma

Guilt

There is a lot of scuttlebutt in the addictions field about trauma. Some of you might have the impression that to deal with your addiction you are going to have to "open up that can of worms," and deal with all your old emotions. Nothing could be further from the truth.

One of the reasons I send women with food addictions (since I collaborate with men) to Dr. Glenn Livingston's *Never Binge Again* is because he refreshingly makes it clear they do not have to sort out deep emotions to get started getting food consumption under control. I feel the same way about all addictions, and that comes from experience both personal and professional. Begin with choosing confidence over fear. Build confidence at your own pace in your own way, and it will grow.

I am also not keen on labels, and I do not buy the disease concept of addiction. None of you reading this is helpless in the face of what is learned behaviour especially as you discover more ahead.

I have enormous respect for those who suffer traumatic events and count myself among them. Yet, the risk for some is it becomes another label, and like the "addiction as a disease" idea, it implies powerlessness and encourages relapse. It says, "I'm addicted because I have trauma, and if I relapse, it's because I have trauma." I cannot think of a less advantageous point of view.

Parents often use guilt to motivate a child to improve a behaviour, using mild emotional extortion to get their darling to conform. Done properly, guilt makes a kid feel uncomfortable and, with parental help, realize a wrong. The brain then has this concept to use going forward. At least that is the hope.

Just the same, high parental expectations mismatched with current ability can result in a confusing emotional backfire in the child, so that guilt is not helpful, but harmful.

Children are not as dumb we think. In his book *Just Babies: The Origins of Good and Evil* Yale University Professor Paul Bloom opens with a tale of three puppets and one-year-olds. A puppet rolls a ball towards another puppet, and that puppet rolls the ball back. Then the puppet rolls the ball to the remaining puppet, and that puppet fucks off with the ball.

The well behaved and poorly behaved puppets are lined up with a cookie in front of each of them for the kid ... and the little one is invited to grab a cookie from the puppet of their choice. Most of the time, the kid takes the cookie from the misbehaving puppet.

Bloom says kids know what justice is early on. They have a capacity for compassion and empathy as well as a rudimentary moral compass set up for their survival amongst others. I suppose this all jives with Gyorgy Buzsáki's inside-out theory, which says the brain is preconfigured for actions and perception because even a one-year-old has had time to notice and verify how things ought to be.

Kids experience families physically, says Mark Peysha from *Robbins-Madanes Training*. I know from experience that when parents or teachers or other caregivers act unfairly, kids might not verbalize their protestations very well, but it still registers in their nervous system.

Every child needs at least one person to whom they can turn for safety and comfort and to whom they can fearlessly reveal themselves and find unconditional acceptance. When a caregiver shows rigid disdain for a child's behaviour, children have to align with their benefactors. They will at first resist but eventually tend to adopt the parent's rejection of that part of themselves.

Shame

Absent an "angel of mercy," as Gabor Mate calls an accepting caregiver, a child is cast adrift from those whom he or she relies upon for succor. This grows what Carl Jung calls the shadow, the parts of the self holding malevolence and which we keep hidden from others.

Over time it also tends to instill shame, so the child feels separated from others and, in some capacity, deficient in comparison to his peers. A child may dissociate from his thoughts and feelings to cope with intense conflict, becoming divorced from his inner self, the psyche fracturing into parts to get by.

We are people makers, said Virginia Satir, and every living thing has a life plan, added Erik Erickson. Since people arrive with only an inborn temperament, it is environmental influences that create Jung's shadow, muting a person's potential by degrees in the process.

Since the brain learns from experience, the early years can wire the child's developing nervous system for protection over connection. Most children will emerge from a family's imperfections and grow into more or less stable adults. Some, however, function well enough but default to an over-reliance on a protective nervous system. A few will develop a personality disorder… which despite the risk of harm to themselves, others, and society, is always an adaptation.

Dealing with shame involves noticing how it shows up in daily life and responding differently. For example, shame produces significant defensiveness as a distrusting spirit's hypervigilance fights off perceived attacks on the soul. Often this means not brokering either criticism or compliment.

"Nice suit," someone says. You answer, "It's outdated." "Good work," someone says. "I'm just doing my job," you answer. Someone says, "Your work is sub-par," triggering protests and an internal war…

By practicing saying thank you to any and all feedback, good or bad, you open the door to learning and connection instead of responding from your feed-fuck-kill-run-hide nervous system (the wolf).

Taking on a parent's disdain as a youngster, however, means creating mistaken beliefs about yourself while ensuring a part of you remains out of reach. "I believe this; therefore, I am that" thinking formed in childhood can perpetuate shame for decades. Carl Jung taught that placing aspects of the self in shadow also tends to hide some of your good parts because the psychic energy involved does not discriminate. How can you grow a part of you that remains hidden?

Re-introducing yourself to your younger self, listening to his story while acting as your own "angel of mercy," and reassuring and defending that part of you until assimilated with your adult self go a long way towards restoration. Hundreds of men who have taken my "Taming Shame" course agree.

Given my earlier comments about labeling yourself as traumatised, I will keep this simple: the secret to success is cooperation. No one makes it on their own. We are "herd animals," as Roy Baumeister says on a Suzanne Venker podcast, and that meta-analysis he did with Mark Leary in the 90s found the need to belong runs the emotional system. Dana and Stephen Porges showed we achieve internal balance (homeostasis) through social engagement.

Trauma

In Baumeister's book with John Tierney, *The Power of Bad*, they write how an estimated 50% of people suffer trauma at some point and most do not get post-traumatic syndrome (PTSD). Furthermore, from 60 to 90% actually experience post-traumatic growth, including those who had PTSD symptoms.

Post-traumatic growth often means more gratitude, better life priorities and relationships, and feeling like you can manage anything. If you want to change how you feel, live new experiences by changing what you do and how you think. That includes questioning beliefs about yourself that are wrong.

We tend to think of successful people as self-starters but that's mostly myth. So says resilience researcher and Dalhousie University Professor Michael Ungar in his book, *Change the World*, pointing out that resilience usually means the wise use of nearby resources.

Change some things about yourself by claiming a higher identity and refusing to cede control to the lower order nervous system (the wolf) but pay attention to environmental factors too. That is why geographic cures work. A guy takes a job in a far-off city and turns his life around. People divorce and years later find happiness with someone new. A change of scenery can work magic.

Ungar says change yourself, your direction, the world around you, or what you want to solve problems.

Too much talk therapy can be a rabbit hole. None of it is needed to quit an addiction. What you do need is to learn new things while implementing action strategies to get functioning as fast as you can. You need to retrain your nervous system to be healthy instead of sick. Choose confidence over fear.

Remember, addiction is ceding control of your being to the body and circumstances to narrow focus and lessen stress. Recovery is about being, imagining who you want to be and then going out and becoming that person. If you stumble, then it may mean you need to go deeper. But you will have built some currency in your stress vs confidence account from time spent breaking old habits and living differently.

For a time when I was much younger my now deceased father used to beat me and my siblings with a hockey stick handle. I got the family record when I was eight years old for tossing a childish note back to Junior, my school classmate, in grade three. Dad took full adult swings with hard Canadian maple while I hung on to a bedpost with my pants down. At 30 strikes I began to fall to the floor each time and plead for mercy. He hit me forty-two more times and changed my life.

For explicit memories you find bothersome, try writing about it. On consecutive days or weeks write free-hand and dump your thoughts and feelings on paper or on a saved document on your computer.

Step 1. Write what happened and why it happened.

Step 2. Review and write about any lessons or hidden benefits not considered before.

Step 3. Write about how this experience has made you stronger than you would have been without it. If you do not see that yet, imagine and write what that will feel like when it does.

Step 4. Create a new meaningful story that includes your nobility in transcending this event.

Step 5. Contrast the why and lessons learned with the precious power and wisdom gained and share with someone you trust. Now, let it go… even if only a little bit.

Then each time it comes to mind… let it go some more. Some men draft a story as per above and burn it in a campfire or fireplace. Use whatever ritual comes to mind. You can minister healing to yourself.

The idea is to bracket this episode, placing a boundary of understanding and acceptance around it so that it doesn't follow you for all time. You are using memory reconsolidation to achieve fear extinction, a process whereby you replace a painful memory with another more acceptable one. You are less likely to be blindsided with emotion later by doing this work now. You stop getting "hooked" by it.

After I drafted the story I call "The Record," I rewrote it several times over the next year or two until I got it right. Rather than a tragic figure, the eventual ending I wrote saw me as a noble figure holding the family record for hits with the hockey stick handle (my brothers counted), and a "better me than them" heroic martyrdom. Then I shared it, and rarely looked at it again. Even when I send it to someone, I do not re-edit like I usually do most things I write.

I read University of Virginia professor Timothy Wilson's book *Redirect* a few years later and realized I had done my own version of the Pennebaker writing exercise, which is remarkably similar and has good science behind it.

I know it works, and those beatings at my father's hand undoubtedly prepared my nervous system to survive being shot, stabbed, run over, hit with baseball bats, and many fights later when I was out on my own. It becomes a chicken and egg thing. I can also surmise none of those things would have happened without that intensive nervous system training.

I won't cover ACE scores much here. Ace stands for Acquired Childhood Experiences, a study by Kaiser Permanente and the CDC which found kids who had a score of four (out of ten) or higher have a greater likelihood of heart disease, obesity, addictions, etc. I score a weak four. You can look them up for more information and take the test online. I definitely meet fear at a different level than most people. This is true of most of my clients. We will cover more of this later in a chapter on stress.

Even the counselling process will cover the four elements of the above writing exercise over a longer timeline. Remember if you feel something today, you have felt it before. If you are able to trace your present-day discomfort to its source in your history, you get a shot at extending yourself a little compassion and, more importantly, reframing limiting beliefs that resulted from your experience.

You may also experience something called catharsis, an intense release of feelings. The injustice I felt at being beaten black and blue from elbows to knees for returning a note to Junior with the word "caca" on it meant I had become stuck in "fight" of flight or flight. This happens to the best of us. Released feelings make way for something else instead of renting space in your psyche long term.

Catharsis can be helpful in situations where the body is stuck between survive and thrive because of some past event still controlling aspects of the nervous system. Evidence for this shows up when you are triggered by something in the present and your reaction does not fit the context. Then go deeper.

I like the Peter Levine type body work stuff because it coincides nicely with mindfulness, something anyone with a nervous system geared toward protection will need to practice on some level to retrain themselves for confidence over fear. Yoga is good, and Deb Dana's exercises are really helpful. Judith Blackstone's Unbound Body book of exercises is also listed below in the resources.

Gabor Mate's "Compassionate Inquiry" helps connect the dots, and all of his books are good. Jeffrey Young's "Schema Therapy" is worthwhile, and everyone can benefit from reading *Reinventing Your Life*.

Sometimes, if enough people call you a horse, it is time to get a saddle. So, for stubborn beliefs and personality disorders (repeats same mistakes, blames others), Montreal psychiatrist Habib Davanloo created "Short-term Dynamic Psychotherapy," of which I'm a fan. Find practitioners all over.

The measure of progress is confidence over fear with a caveat. I am reminded of one of Baumeister's books, *Willpower*, when he had a change of heart regarding the self esteem movement and embraced discipline as a pathway to a successful life. He said if you help an asshole gain self-esteem, you wind up with a high self-esteem asshole (or words to that effect). Make sure you build best-self confidence.

In my case, watching crying children used to hurt; knowing a child was being hit made my blood boil. Now, it simmers. A former gangster, I evolved to claim justice as one of my top values.

You are run by your nervous system with conscious awareness along for the ride.

For example, it was not until I was studying behavioural sciences in college that I realized, being out of the house as a teenager, drifting into alliances with gangsters and drug dealers a few years my senior was an effort to replace two older brothers missing from my life. Meanwhile, given my experiences with my father, I could not trust men or authority. That took longer to unravel and figure out.

If you are able to do some of these things, you have my congratulations. Pain is there to teach us, and you will have made your suffering pay...

Summaries

You don't have to solve complex feelings to abstain from an addiction.

You don't have a disease; you are not helpless in the face of your addiction.

You were born with an innate sense of justice and a capacity for empathy.

Children need an angel of mercy who gives acceptance; adults need someone safe to come home to.

The whole nervous system, including and especially the brain, is trained by experience.

When kids are told they are bad or get that impression, shame grows.

Shame is the sense that you are different than others and maybe even defective.

Trauma creates post-traumatic growth in most people.

To solve my problems, I can change myself, my direction, the world around me, or what I want.

You are run by your nervous system with conscious awareness along for the ride.

Pain is there to teach you. Make your suffering pay.

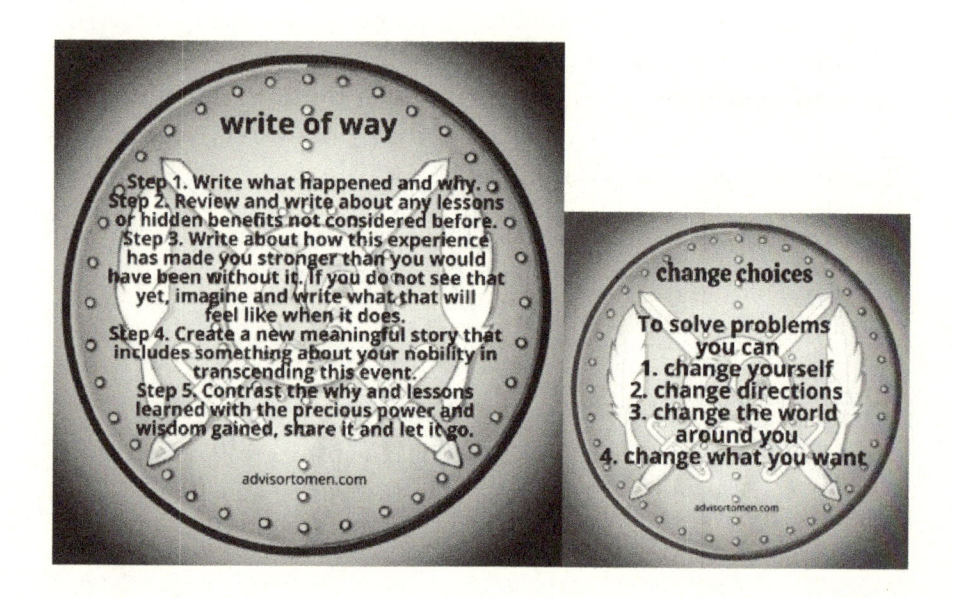

write of way

Step 1. Write what happened and why.
Step 2. Review and write about any lessons or hidden benefits not considered before.
Step 3. Write about how this experience has made you stronger than you would have been without it. If you do not see that yet, imagine and write what that will feel like when it does.
Step 4. Create a new meaningful story that includes something about your nobility in transcending this event.
Step 5. Contrast the why and lessons learned with the precious power and wisdom gained, share it and let it go.

advisortomen.com

change choices

To solve problems you can
1. change yourself
2. change directions
3. change the world around you
4. change what you want

advisortomen.com

9. EMOTIONS

In this chapter I'll discuss:

1. Constructed Emotion

2. The Crazy 8

3. Universal Love

Constructed Emotion

It is from living that I know that repeatedly putting the body into a fear state, absent visible threat, has a cumulative effect on frame of mind, especially confidence. I rely on my reading of science and brilliant neuroscientists, but intuition and experience also inform how I help men defeat their addictions.

Having said all that, let us talk about emotions. Because, to move away from fear and towards more confidence, we must get better at understanding feelings. Do not worry, I will be gentle.

Emotional essentialism contends that we possess a baseline set of feelings, said to be disgust, fear, happiness, sadness, surprise, and anger. These are said to occur automatically in response to what we experience in our environment. This is mistaken.

The idea was that a particular part of the brain governed each of these essential emotions. An example is fear and the amygdala. The amygdala leads, but many parts of the brain participate in an emotion.

Another thing that came along during my time is micro-expressions, no doubt aided by the trend to understand body language. The promise was that you could tell someone's true feelings by scrutinizing involuntary "leakages" of emotion in facial expressions caught by the prepared observer.

We do leak emotion to let each other know what's up. At best it's an indication of something, of what you cannot be sure. So are lie detector machines faulty, which themselves can be gamed.

If you want to know how someone is feeling, it is best to ask them… with the following caveat.

What people say is not a contract with those in their environment but, rather, more of a trial balloon floated amongst others for feedback. Some of us are good at explaining what is on our mind, others not so much. Remember, most of what you think comes from the body.

Add in self concept: how we see ourselves is tied to how we believe others see us. Depending on the context, and/or who is around, you might answer differently from one day to the next even when asked about something factual.

This is critical: if you don't know how you see yourself, if you don't know how you feel, you default to receiving messaging about yourself from outside of you. "The world will ask who you are, and if you don't know, the world will tell you." — Carl Jung

Remember the show *"Who Wants to be a Millionaire"* hosted by Canadian comic Howie Mandel? Contestants could phone a friend or ask the audience for help in answering a question. Asking the audience was rarely wrong. There is a reason for that. The hivemind prevails. It's seductive.

We evolved as "herd animals," according to Roy Baumeister. We are designed for shared thinking. We were never made to go it alone. We use words and tone of voice backed by body position, eye-gaze, and facial expressions to discern what is up with others and let others know what is going on with us, for reassurance, unity, and to meet needs.

We have already gone over how you feel differently when you are hungry versus satiated, tired versus alert, relaxed versus when you are agitated because you need to take a piss, have a cold, or are cold. You are reminded of how your thoughts and feelings change according to your physiology. But how?

Whereas most of us believe we react to people and conditions, in her book *How Emotions Are Made* Lisa Feldman Barrett explains constructed emotion. Turns out the brain operates predictively, not reactively, and that distinction alone can shift a man's perspective. Predictive versus reactive. Remember that.

As explained earlier, from birth a continuous loop of information called interoception happens between brain and body. This creates a sense of how you feel called affect. Barrett points out affect is not quite emotion but broader, and comes in two kinds: valence, and arousal.

Keeping it simple, valence is comfort over discomfort, or pleasant over unpleasant. Arousal is about being alert or relaxed. Becoming aware of this general affective state can help identify triggers to addiction. Clue in to affect early and you can nip fear in the bud and, instead, build confidence.

Your brain uses interoception to predict and adjust your reality to meet the body's demands in various contexts, something Lisa Feldman Barrett calls your body budget, that is, simultaneous measures of energy use, temperature, heart rate, movement, etc.

Buzsaki in *The Inside Out Brain* says, "There is no such thing as unknown for the brain. Every new mountain, river, or situation has elements of familiarity, reflecting previous experiences in similar situations, which can activate one of the pre-existing neuronal trajectories."

"In every waking moment," Feldman-Barrett writes, "your brain uses past experience, organized as concepts, to guide your actions and give your sensations meaning. When the concepts involved are emotion concepts, your brain constructs instances of emotion. Think horse and get one concept, think 'jealousy,' and get another."

Your brain does this in a flash, beneath your awareness, and is only corrected afterwards by social reality. Walk in on pieces of a conversation and you might get the wrong idea of what is being said and be seized with horror, only to listen more intently and see things clarified moments later and relax. That is the brain predictively piecing things together and correcting. Your affective state in any given moment influences how you interpret what is going on around you. Bingo.

More from Feldman-Barrett:

"The theory of constructed emotion incorporates elements of all three flavors of construction. From social construction, it acknowledges the importance of culture and concepts. From psychological construction, it considers emotions to be constructed by core systems in the brain and body. And from neuro construction, it adopts the idea that experience wires the brain."

Just because she can, my daughter Charlie likes to pet bees while they gather pollen from flowering clover. Her school once called to complain she was teaching this skill to her third-grade classmates during recess and asked us to have a talk with her. She rarely gets stung. She thinks bees are "cute and a bit fluffy."

On the other hand, at age seven my son stepped on a ground bees' nest opening while we were clearing brush on an under-used trail. After he was stung, he ran the quarter-mile home to his mom. He is not amused by bees, wasps, hornets, and the like. No, not at all.

My children each have quite different concepts of what "bee" means. As they come in for supper, Charlie is constantly reassuring Howie about the wasps heading to a nest in the back porch soffits. "It's OK, Howie. They are just going home for the night too," she will say. He remains skeptical…

Three ingredients to emotion: interoception (which creates affect), concepts, and social reality. You train your brain through experiential action, and the concepts formed from these actions become what the brain relies upon to make predictions in the future.

Feldman-Barrett suspects addiction is driven by a chronically out of whack body budget. I cover how this happens in chapter 2. I believe putting your body into an aroused state or protection mode in the absence of visible threat confuses the brain at a cost to confidence (at a minimum).

The Crazy 8

When I worked in the newspaper industry, I taught my door-to-door reps that we own three things: our thoughts, our feelings, and our behaviours. Constructed emotions helps you take full responsibility while unequivocally knowing that thinking, feeling, and acting, all begin with you. That is helpful.

Action is the architect of our experience. Constructed emotion confirms that if you feel something today, you have likely felt it before.

But what happens when we find our emotions swinging from one extreme to another? After all, the body is forever trying to rebalance its internal energies in the face of circumstances.

What happens when you get pissed off at someone or a situation, but instead of eventually calming down you go further... and become bummed out?

Then later, you think of that person or situation, and you get riled up all over again. Then you calm down... to sadness. Then you get peeved some more... and maybe you do this over and over until you eventually flirt with depression. It goes the other way too, from sadness to anger and back. This sows the seeds of what is referred to as bipolar.

If you have a nervous system trained more for protection than connection, your attempts to regulate emotion can be all over the place. Without social engagement, homeostasis is in doubt, and you could find yourself becoming activated in this manner indefinitely. We want to avoid this. I learned a great infinity loop visual for this while taking the Robbins-Madanes Training.

It's one of my favourite tools and I have jazzed it up from the basic version I learned almost a decade ago.

My Crazy 8 might seem busy, and that is on purpose. If you decided to save this graphic, I want you to have something to refer to with enough reminders and options on it to provide you with a pause between stimulus and response to help with decision making. Let's go over it.

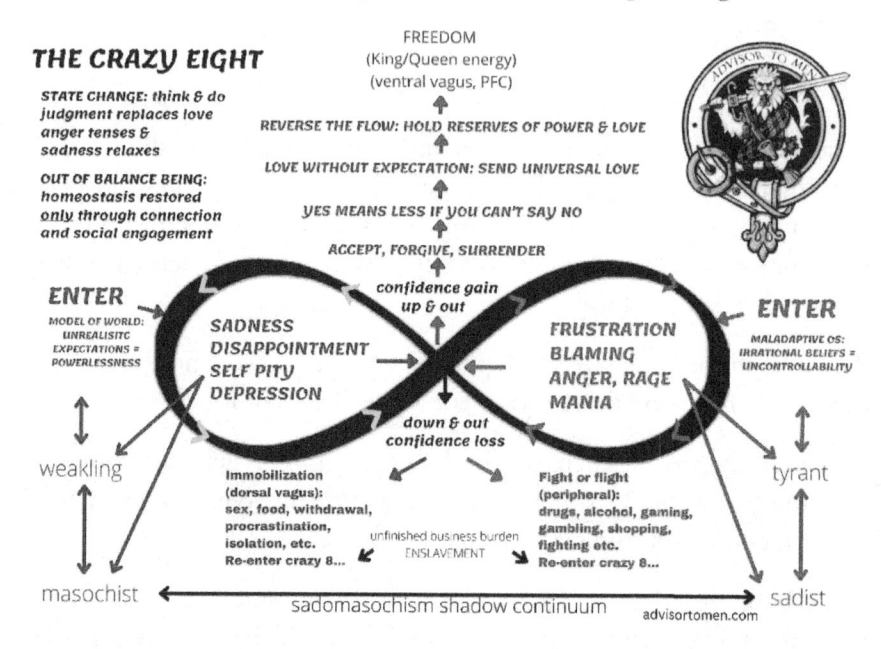

THE CRAZY EIGHT

FREEDOM
(King/Queen energy)
(ventral vagus, PFC)

STATE CHANGE: think & do
judgment replaces love
anger tenses &
sadness relaxes

REVERSE THE FLOW: HOLD RESERVES OF POWER & LOVE

OUT OF BALANCE BEING:
homeostasis restored
only through connection
and social engagement

LOVE WITHOUT EXPECTATION: SEND UNIVERSAL LOVE

YES MEANS LESS IF YOU CAN'T SAY NO

ACCEPT, FORGIVE, SURRENDER

confidence gain
up & out

ENTER
MODEL OF WORLD:
UNREALISTIC
EXPECTATIONS =
POWERLESSNESS

SADNESS
DISAPPOINTMENT
SELF PITY
DEPRESSION

FRUSTRATION
BLAMING
ANGER, RAGE
MANIA

ENTER
MALADAPTIVE OS:
IRRATIONAL BELIEFS =
UNCONTROLLABILITY

down & out
confidence loss

weakling

Immobilization
(dorsal vagus):
sex, food, withdrawal,
procrastination,
isolation, etc.
Re-enter crazy 8...

unfinished business burden
ENSLAVEMENT

Fight or flight
(peripheral):
drugs, alcohol, gaming,
gambling, shopping,
fighting etc.
Re-enter crazy 8...

tyrant

masochist ← sadomasochism shadow continuum → sadist

advisortomen.com

Top left with State Change, I simplify things, so to change state change what you think and/or change what you do implicating focus, how judgment replaces love while anger tenses and sadness relaxes, and mentioning we achieve homeostasis though social engagement and connection.

You can enter on either side of the Crazy 8 variously by way of irrational beliefs and/or unrealistic expectations. These both tend to create powerlessness, often where the general contributors to psychological stress like novelty, uncertainty, and uncontrollability compound and become exaggerated.

If you are bouncing back and forth in a Crazy 8, clearly your model of the world is not working. You must escape the Crazy 8 and you can go out through the top or through the bottom. First, the bottom, which is like the revolving door of a self-imposed prison, there for incarcerated recidivist ruminators.

Thus, the down and out is where confidence goes to die. I differentiate between dorsal vagus immobilization, feed and digestion, and peripheral nervous system fight or flight (I skip fawn as a men's counsellor). I show how these strategies are temporary fixes which invite re-entry into the Crazy 8.

I include the archetypal passive and active shadows of the warrior, self pity (masochism) and blaming (sadism), and the active and passive King energies of tyrant and weakling abdicator (see House of Lannister last 2 kings on "Game of Thrones" for examples). For more on archetypes of male maturation, a good book for men is *King, Warrior, Magician, Lover* (1990) by Jungian analysts Moore and Gillette.

Out of the Crazy 8 topside, where confidence flourishes, "accept, forgive, surrender" is something an ex-brother-in-law said to me regarding his wife's sister. He wanted me to apply it to my relationship and fix it. Despite his good intentions, I had been several years divorced by then, so I thanked him, applied it to myself, and healed. It is a useful mantra I still teach. She died recently, tragically too young, bless her.

Scarcity drives value, be it oil, diamonds… or yesses. I suggest men get used to starting with no (see also chapter 3, "Wanting"), and to say no often… and yes only sometimes. A good line to use is, "Give me a reason to say yes." Then, given a reason, consider delaying your decision overnight if you can.

Universal Love

I am not a fan of unconditional love. We can muster it in the moment, but otherwise, it is fool's gold. Better to be powerful enough to give because you can. Expectations drive our disappointments.

Use your imagination and try this with me: realize and accept that love exists in the world, in fact, it is all around you. Now see yourself gathering up some of that love energy and concentrating it in your sternum region. Next picture yourself sending love out to whoever pissed you off as electric love emanating from your fingers like a comic book superhero.

Among other places, I learned to do this driving 80,000 kilometers per year in big cities across Canada, often during rush hour. I would get cut off and find myself activated. So, I would start by saying, "I send you love mother fucker!" By the second or third time, it was just, "I send you love..."

This allows an escape out the top from the sadism (blaming) or masochism (self-pity) of the Crazy 8. Sending love is incompatible with hatred, anger, or sadness. Think that might build confidence?

By summoning feelings which may be ordinarily vague, you are tying them back to your inner life, letting yourself know that these are indeed part of you. Practicing this is tremendously empowering.

In my view, we do not mature emotionally as men until we stop looking for love. I source the need for love in remnant childhood wishes for parental positive regard. Truth is, you have generations of father's power and mother's love within you and can use these ancestral reserves in service of those whom you defend while expanding meaning and freedom.

By ascending further, you activate the ventral vagus social engagement and satisfy your inescapable need to belong. Rather than cede control to the body and circumstances, you live out your higher values in support of a fully claimed identity.

You assume your King energetic state. Again, referencing Moore and Gillette, King energy handles order and fertility and blessings. You cannot have a kingdom without order, nor is a fertile king easily usurped or overthrown. Benevolent kings bless people, which you can do by seeing the good in others, often before they can see it themselves, and letting them know. A person who uses their power and love in service of self and others finds meaning and freedom.

No doubt you have benefitted from taking the time to "center" yourself for a moment before continuing at something challenging. Andrew Huberman suggests using the metaphor of a seesaw to describe the alert and relaxed state of the body. He pinpoints the insula in the brain as the registrar and interpreter of bodily signaling which it then reports to the left dorsolateral prefrontal cortex which acts as the hinge screw to turn up or down this activation. As mentioned in an earlier chapter, it is here you can pause and mind the "gap" and turn your anxiety into curiousity and exploration, during which time PFC will direct the vagus nerve to slow the heart rate and calm you down.

Everyone needs predictability, though you are now mindful that comfort zones are places where dreams go to die. Entropy, the second law of thermodynamics, says any system left alone will decay. In case you missed the message, you expand, or you die, so get moving. Look after basics but push through your resistance to become more by embracing uncertainty when you are called to grow. This is how you build confidence and displace fear, through the action perception loop.

Sometimes a Crazy 8 cycle is about connecting with your own body. Anger tenses and sadness relaxes. What if instead of meeting your needs this way, you tried something else? How about exploring how you can connect with others however you can.

Who would you need to be to rise up and out?

If you want new feelings, you must live new experiences.

Summaries

We are herd animals, using body, voice, face, and eye-gaze to reassure each other.

The brain is predictive, not reactive.

There is no such thing as unknown to the brain; everything is compared to what it knows already.

Interoception, affect, concepts, and social reality construct emotion.

When the brain forms poor concepts under addiction, confusion and low confidence results.

If you feel something today, you have felt it before.

Give me a good reason to say yes.

You can't send someone love and hate at the same time, so send love and be free.

10. DEPRESSION

In this chapter I'll discuss:

1. Normal Depression

2. Meds, Renewal, & The Hero's Journey

3. Re-Purpose

Normal Depression

I have felt this gloom we call depression and I have gone deep with it: sadness, emptiness, a subdued lifeforce, appetite changes, sleep changes, sluggishness, loss of meaning, distraction, suicidal thoughts.

Years ago, I found myself in a values conflict with the principals of a company where I worked. I loved providing solutions to customers but disagreed with the owner's approach to the market and me in particular. Because I have a wife and kids to support, I continued at the job long past when I should have. I had hoped an opportunity would present itself to do what I do best, which is to mentor and build teams. It was not going to happen. I felt led on and trapped, and I grew depressed.

A second time, I finally caught Covid. First week symptoms were simple head congestion, except one night when I shivered for four hours. The second week symptoms lessened, replaced by an overwhelming sadness I cannot explain. It was as if a dark veil of gloom had descended upon my world despite having no dissatisfaction in my personal or professional life that I could point to as its cause.

In the first scenario, my depression lasted a year. During that time, I did not work out as I usually do. I craved carbs and ate sweets more often too. I slowed down, plodding along, careful, and deliberate.

I slept much more, often nine hours per night after being a seven hour per night guy for thirty plus years. The bi-phasic sleep I am accustomed to from a lifetime of waking in the middle of the night and reading for an hour was often absent. I slept right through it almost half the time and had trouble getting up and facing the morning, despite a thirty-year waking-up routine that usually sets up my day.

I soldiered on because that is what people do. Some eat more, sleep more, worry more when depressed. Some do not. Some lose weight, lose sleep, and still worry.

Furthermore, in short order I knew I was depressed. I did not talk about it to missus, though I am sure she knew. Men were my confidants; it was to these few I turned as I searched for answers. I sought to realign my life in response to my physical signaling.

You see, I knew what was going on, lucky to have that kind of awareness.

If you feel depressed you must realize your depression is a normal thing. People sometimes get hung up on the issue of depression and think it means they are broken, that there is something wrong with them, that there is a "normal" out there and by some accident of fate, they do not fit the bill.

Of course, feeling like that is deceptive, and is more likely shame than depression. "It must be me" is not only bullshit we tell ourselves, but also often the same bullshit implied by others. It is a chicken and egg thing: did my depression cause my chemical imbalance or did my chemical imbalance cause my depression? The idea is more like a dog chasing its tail. I have used that simile before.

Every year, the Mental Health Awareness Week folks remind us that one in five adults will have a MAJOR depressive episode in their lifetime.

That is a big chunk of us. So, if 20% of the population gets a big depression at some point, you can bet many of the rest of folks feel depressed at some level at some time too. I would take those odds.

This is proof of depression as natural, though hardly optimal. This psychological mechanism has survived thousands of years of evolution for a reason. Traits only stick around because they are needed. So many of us would not become depressed if it did not serve an important function.

Meds, Renewal, and The Hero's Journey

If you feel a depression lingering, check in with your doctor, as they are best qualified to assess and recommend treatment. Meds or no meds? Well, if you have a job that you like, family and friends you enjoy, a few hobbies, and you are still depressed, meds will probably help. But do not stop there.

If you have none of those things, meds will help but lifestyle changes must be part of the solution.

I once listened to the head of psychiatry at the University of Toronto on a CBC radio show speak about how meds are only effective short term. The body gets used to them, and then you have to adjust dosage strength and eventually even try some other brand or formulation. How many of us know someone on antidepressants for a decade or longer?

If you do go on meds and they are working, consider your meds have bought you time to make changes, not solved your problem. Otherwise, they are another drug addiction. No confidence to be had there.

Then there's grief. People can become depressed after the loss of a loved one. Grief has that effect on most of us, though almost all return to a version of normal within a year. A few take heartbreak and refuse to let it go. I send them heart-felt blessings of power and love.

Douglas Hofstadter writes about how we exist in each other in his book *A Strange Loop*. The idea that you are over there, and I am over here, is an inadequate way to describe us. Losing a loved one means that part of us that exists in them is in doubt. This shatters our trust in the world, our belonging paradigm forever altered. An albeit imperfect balance might be achieved by realizing where they exist in you is never gone. The departed echo endlessly down through time in those who knew them.

It is an honourable process. I'm paraphrasing from memory what Hofstadter wrote about losing his wife. I am grateful to him for sharing how he tried his best to make sense of it. I have used his ideas to deal with my own grief and to sympathize with the grieving of others countless times since.

Addictions make grieving worse. Far better to honour the deceased by living a good life.

Depression is also your signal to look at your model of the world and give it a tune-up. Something is not working for you and needs your profound attention. It may need a complete overhaul and rebuild. Something may need to cease or be abandoned, or at least be reborn as something else. That is what depression is, and there is no need to conflate it beyond this powerful simplicity. How you understand your world and operate within it is what is broken, not you.

So, what does the body do in this case? Besides experiencing lethargy with sleep and eating affected, we turn inwards as a great introspection of doubt and questioning occurs. Omphaloskepsis is how I like to think of it: metaphorically, navel gazing. Our thinking slows as well, often looping, like a skipping record, and usually becoming narrower in scope as we fixate on the things which cause us pain. We may be so enamored with our suffering that we actively turn away from happiness.

No one fixes another's depression. Just as it is true, we do depression rather than it does us.

We may think positively, telling ourselves we really ought to lighten up, but for all our cognitive steering, the body does not seem to follow. At least, not right away. That is because the body is where your feelings lie. The soul must be in the body, linking all of your organs but particularly the heart and the belly, connected to the brain by the vagus.

It is trite to say we are all on a journey but call it what you wish. Depression is the dark night of the soul in your hero's journey. Working your way through addiction is a hero's journey. The American mythologist Joseph Campbell said we go through a series of these throughout life. Steven Barnes taught me this condensed version of the journey, and you may recognize these steps of ancestral myth:

1. Hero confronted with challenge

2. Rejects challenge

3. Accepts challenge

4. Road of trials

5. Gathering allies and gaining powers

6. Confront evil and defeated

7. Dark night of the soul

8. The leap of faith

9. Confronts evil and victorious

10. Student becomes teacher

Number 7 is a tough step. It is a black cloud of doubt and immobility. A seeming hopelessness sets in so that the affected person is rubbed painfully and even cruelly into the mire. It is purposeful torment, though it's hard to see it this way. Pain teaches. Make your suffering pay.

It is like when you dove too deeply in water as a child and were running out of air. You looked up and saw the light at the surface, and it was a race to kick your way to oxygen before you passed out and drowned. You give it all your might. Every ounce of your body and will combined act in the effort.

It is like when the bully has you pinned down and is slapping your face and, miraculously, you find power you did not know you had to buck him off and escape.

It is sourced from the same stuff as when a person finds the superhuman power to lift a car off a loved one after an accident in an act of hysterical strength. Not the weakened alcohol-fueled version of manufactured fear used by Paul in the introduction. It is an agonizing call to reach deep and try hard. It is a silent scream inside us that says "NO."

How many times have you been pushed into danger, into a situation where you felt like your survival was in question, yet somehow found inside you the resources to overcome and live? Pushed to grow, by some means you continued.

Re-Purpose

With depression, we are called to grow once again; it is complacency we should curse. Most addictions are life at a kind of emotional standstill, and like the dog chasing the tail, going nowhere fast.

That is what depression is. It is the universe tantalizingly telling you to adapt. It is demanding change. It is saying you are coming up short, that the life bestowed upon you is under threat, and it demands your care. It screams at you for adjustments, and lets you know through the whole chain of your being, interoception-concept-prediction, with pain, confusion, darkness, and hopelessness.

She is a hard taskmistress, our universe. There are a billion stars in the Andromeda Galaxy I like to remind people. Best not fuck with that kind of force. Like a child demanding attention, depression is a temper tantrum of the soul.

It is a test of your balls. It is a doubter. It is the take-away closer who says, "Maybe this isn't for you." It is a push at your boundaries of tolerance, demanding a greater integration of your parts. It is nature calling you, provocatively wondering if you have what it takes to stand up for yourself and make the declaration, "THE PAIN STOPS HERE!"

Like confidence, depression can be lifted from one big change or a series of small things which add up to a retooling of your model of the world. Sometimes changing jobs, moving to a new city, or leaving or gaining a relationship allows the light of renewal to shine in. But that is rarely enough.

At other times, these are temporary because the internal operating model is what needs attention. In my case I realized I was compromising my life and gifts to satisfy responsibilities to others. I realize I do this as a tendency, having done it most of my life. And of course, I could source this to an abandonment fear as a child, to a deep toxic shame from my early years as someone broken and never good enough.

My method was to become more so as to convince myself and others around me I was worthwhile. This nice guy strategy works... until it does not. (See reference to Robert Glover's book *No More Mr. Nice Guy* below). Now depression told me it was time to reparent myself; no one was going to do it for me. I needed to change jobs and set limits to keep my sanity. So, I did.

In my second example, on the Monday of the third week post-Covid my sadness lifted. It was all interoception and, as my body fought off the virus, so did I defeat depression.

In the first example, it took a year to recover, during which I worked at a failed start up, which continues to fail. I put two traction plans before management, and both were turned down. I left, pissed at first, but used the Crazy 8 strategies, and in short order I was fine. I sent that fucker love. Ha!

I was not depressed any longer, though. I was alive and felt it. And I got stronger as I went along. I decided to do my best to live my purpose. I had always counselled people but decided to expand this part of my life while taking a real estate course. Within three months I dropped the real estate idea completely and have only become busier.

Almost three years later, I am the happiest I have ever been because I decided I would be. It was one part decision and another part purpose recipe. Addiction for me is in the past. It can be for you too.

I accepted that each of us is chosen for life by heavens of infinite wisdom and that our purpose is to take whatever meagre talents have been accorded us and use them to make a difference nearby, expanding meaning and freedom until we find our place in the sun. That is, it!

Knowing all this, if you are prone to doing depression and now feeling your pain as a signal for change, what is one tiny step you could take? Just one thing, one little change in what you think or what you do. Think and do. Start there. Move.

In his book *Flourish*, Martin Seligman says to write down three positive things at the end of each day and why they happened. Why not do that practice permanently, as it seems to work better than antidepressants.

Rome was not built in a day. Our expectations drive all of our disappointments. Change one thing, then another, then one more… Soon you will have a direction. You will build momentum. This is how we defeat addiction or depression or make any big change. Incremental improvement builds confidence.

You will know if it is right for you because your body will tell you. Our eyes may see out but somehow you will see the fog within begin to lift.

When a sense of harmony among others is lived consistently, we go confidently into the night. We are inter-connected and ready to meet challenges, putting order to chaos while visiting awe and expressing the gifts given to us by life. Self-concept is destiny.

Ask yourself: what shall I do in my metamorphosis?

How will I emerge when I am done?

This is your act of creation.

Summaries

Depression is normal, that is why nature has kept it around.

Meds don't solve problems, but they may buy you time to make a change in thinking.

Where I existed in someone may come into doubt, but where they exist in me is never in question.

We exist in each other; the departed echo down through time in those left behind.

We do depression as much as it does us.

Only you can fix your depression.

Depression is a temper tantrum of the soul.

Depression calls us to grow; it is complacency we should curse.

She's a hard taskmaster, our universe. There are a billion stars in the Andromeda galaxy alone.

Nature calls you, provocatively, wondering if you have what it takes to declare "the pain stops here."

Depression can be lifted by one big change or a series of small ones to retool your model of the world. Use gratitude liberally.

Consistent harmony with those around us means we go confidently into the night.

Ask: What shall I do with my metamorphosis?

*Note: psychedelics are mentioned in the next chapter, ANXIETY

11. ANXIETY

In this chapter I'll discuss:

1. Describing anxiety

2. Attachment Threat Cycle

3. Countering Strategies

Describing Anxiety

Anxious people often turn to various addictions to cope with their discomfort, so I want to give you some tools to use if that happens to you. I wish I could tell you otherwise, but you cannot get rid of anxiety, at least not completely. I am not sure that the scientific community has achieved real consensus on its source either. To my mind, it is a blessing and a curse derived from being able to remember yesterday and imagine tomorrow.

Anxiety is caused by a real or perceived threat to wellbeing and most of the time manifests itself subconsciously making it a little tricky. It is those three broad stress triggers, novelty, uncertainty, and uncontrollability, giving rise to a sense of powerlessness, which are usually at play.

Anxiety often happens when we are conflicted about things. It happens when possibilities are uncertain but also when morality, desires, relationships, and circumstances pull us in two directions, towards and away, where we are of two minds about things. Simultaneously wanting and not wanting or loving and hating is confusing to the predictive brain.

For these reasons, I tend to describe anxiety as a temporary loss of faith in the future. Andrew Huberman says anxiety is a bias towards action. We should take that as encouragement.

If you have ever used or needed an excuse to engage in an addiction, the stress of avoiding anxiety is on a personal been-there-done-that list. Because anxiety is felt at an existential level, it is the lower order nervous system which first mounts a defence. The wolf moves to take over.

It is usually felt in the body as agitation and appears in the mind as confusion. The usual way we solve problems is not working and, imperceptibly, we begin to breathe shallower and more often. The feed-fuck-kill-run-hide wolf has begun to circle...

After a time, your chest tightens up uncomfortably. It can be mild all the way to feeling like something has a grip on your diaphragm and is squeezing hard. Of course, once this is noticed we freak out a little and over-breathe more. Soon we are in an escalating body-brain fear loop.

Those physical sensations are real, and they beget matching catastrophizing thoughts because the brain follows action. Remember, if the body is on alert, the brain will use your databank of prior experience concepts to predictively create a story which matches your physiology. Soon you are compounding your physical discomfort with more thoughts of alarm which, of course, makes you act out the loop by further pacing and breathing commensurately to cope.

The first time I felt it in the 1980s, I was in a drug recovery home when the gravity of fifteen years of dysfunctional living closed in on me with high uncertainty. I thought I was having a heart attack. At the hospital emergency I was put through tests, and the doc came out and said that my gullet was flipping. My Canadian politeness intact, I thanked him and asked for an explanation. When he told me I was having an anxiety attack... well, I cannot tell you how disappointed I was.

Oh, I had felt plenty of fear deep in my body before, from so many times anticipating my father's wrath and my mother's disapproval as a young boy, to the cat-and mouse-games with police and the criminal element later on, but always in the face of real danger. Yet, here I was, relatively safe, yet my usually reliable adversity system had let me down. I also wasn't turning to addictions to change my state.

The following basics will help you better understand anxiety.

You will remember from an earlier chapter Paul Bloom's experiment in which, given a choice, one-year-olds will mostly take a cookie from a misbehaved puppet. This is believed to be the child meting out a punishment to the uncooperative puppet. One kid wanders over, takes a cookie, and gives the bad puppet a smack upside the head for extra emphasis. Bloom argues that you have an internal sense of justice from the outset of life.

The Baumeister and Leary 1995 attachment meta-analysis found *the need to belong* "operated in every corner of a person's psyche and all manner of their behaviour." The emotional system is governed by our need for connection (broadly: connect = feel good, disconnect = feel bad). When connection is in doubt, the body reacts and moves into protection mode.

Recall how we see ourselves is unavoidably contrasted with how we believe others see us, so a clash of self concept will often produce anxiety. If you view yourself as honest and tell a lie, unless you are personality disordered (itself an adaptation), you will experience cognitive dissonance. You can take the path of least resistance and rationalize your weakness and suffer a downgrade in self concept. Or you own up to your mistake and retain and strengthen the view you have of yourself.

The eminent psychiatrist George Vaillant ran the Grant/Gluek study for decades. It was started between 1938 and 1945 and tracked close to 700 Harvard and inner-city Boston men with extensive interviews that included their physicians every two years for life.

Of the three books Valliant wrote on the study, *Triumphs of Experience* was the last. In it, he revealed the obvious things like smoking and drinking kills. He is famous for having said "Happiness is love, full stop," and showed how warm relations were associated with higher earnings.

Poor maternal relations saw a four-fold increase in dementia. Warm paternal relationships meant less adult anxiety, more fun on holidays, and life satisfaction at age 75. My dad said his folks broke his heart.

The Attachment Threat Cycle

What got my attention was how Vaillant studied ego defenses used by the men to cope with life and how these evolved from immature defenses to mature defenses as they aged.

The integrated nervous system (ego in Freudian terms) referees between lower drives and the values and identity influenced executive function of higher-order thinking. In a related book, *The Wisdom of the Ego*, Vaillant writes of how we *"deny, distort, and repress inner and/or outer reality to lessen anxiety and depression."* Understanding attachment and ego defenses exposes the root of anxiety and can change the way you deal with stress. Deal with stress and soon addiction is unnecessary.

You will remember Polyvagal Theory and the ventral vagus facilitating social engagement and reassurance (heart, lungs, throat, voice, facial expression). Ventral activation connects you with yourself, the world, your spirit, and especially others.

I like to explain Vaillant and others' work around ego defenses as the "attachment threat cycle," presented below in a graphic I use to teach the concepts. By understanding this cycle and where you might have picked up an imperfect model of the world, you gain deep understanding. I'm also betting that as you understand this in yourself, you will gain greater compassion for others.

ATTACHMENT THREAT CYCLE

THREAT

=+hypervigilance
=+defensiveness

SADNESS/GRIEF
= imperfect survival

FEAR
threat triggers =
belonging
wants
morals
events

CONSOLIDATION
= acceptance of new reality

BELONGING WANTS
MORALITY EVENTS
^EGO TRIGGERS^
internal/external

CONFLICT
= "of two minds"
= push/pull body

LESS ANXIETY
= ecological self-regulation

psychotic
immature
intermediate
mature

ANXIETY
= loss of faith in future

EGO DEFENSES

Based on Valliant, Wisdom of the Ego
advisortomen.com

Let us use a mild example. A mom tells a five-year-old kid he is going to have to go to a neighbours' house for the afternoon while she runs errands. The kid has never been to the neighbours' before and does not want to go. This makes him afraid, so his sense of fairness kicks in, and he protests while looking for reassurance. His mother persists, and so he is forced into a dual position of both loving his mother and being angry at her. This "two minds" condition is compounded by a "push/pull" in his body and is felt as anxiety. Faith in his future is now in doubt: novelty, uncertainty, uncontrollability.

What can a five-year-old do against an adult? This is when ego defenses come into play.

He might act out and cause a big fuss. He could create a story to justify staying with Mom or manufacture a belief about himself. He could shut down his thoughts and feelings, subjugating himself to circumstances. He could get a tummy ache and try to get Mom to stay home and nurse him. He could be a nuisance at the neighbours in an "I told you not to leave me here" comeuppance. He might tell his mom that the neighbour did not like him and prefers that mom never leave him there again.

These basic defenses, acting out, retreating into make-believe, dissociation, hypochondriasis, passive aggressiveness, and projection function as ecological self-regulation in the child to keep anxiety in check. In the case of a child resisting day care several times per week, the defenses might consolidate as the helpless kid is forced to accept a new reality.

In our example, the original attachment threat remains unaddressed to the nervous system's satisfaction. His use of ego defenses does not assuage his fear and he's now left with an imperfect survival, a forced one. The result is a lingering sadness or even a subconscious grief.

All around you, people operate with irreconciled attachment threats and cope as best they can. You, me, everybody. In particular, children who are significantly conflicted may use dissociation, shutting down thoughts and feelings to get through a crisis. This divorces him from his inner life in subjugation to parental authority. As an adult later, he may avoid emotional closeness and hide it in various ways (perhaps like Paul from the introduction who uses booze to socialize).

Dissociation may compromise his memory and leave part of him in shadow. He may be unable to connect with himself. As an adult, asked how he really feels, he may have no real idea and, instead, guesses. If that is you, in part or in whole, the good news is that, unlike Humpty Dumpty, you are not broken and can be put back together again by retraining your nervous system.

As I often say, ostracism is the real scourge of mankind. Repressed emotion in men has quality of life and even life and death consequences. We must get better at connecting, and to do that we need to be better at knowing how we feel. Emotional granularity means being able to describe precisely your emotional state, using a variety of feeling words. People with emotional granularity see the doctor less often says Lisa Feldman Barrett. That tells you plenty.

As our five-year-old grows into an adult, to his detriment he may become hypervigilant and highly defensive to criticism as his ego fends off perceived threats to wellbeing and belonging (in defense of the soul). His nervous system may become stoked for protection over connection. He is forced to hide parts of himself he deems unacceptable to his caregivers.

Worse, in his subconscious grief he learns to avoid emotional closeness using various tactical defenses, such as exaggeration, confusion, intellectualization, reliance on jargon, indirect speech, forgetfulness, denial, pig-headedness, closed body language, and more.

Fully grown, he may have a disagreement with someone at work and find all the bad drivers suddenly show up on his commute home. When he speaks, his language is devoid of feeling words, and he prefers intellect over emotion. He once got into a significant accident on the freeway in which no one was hurt. Instead of being rattled by it as you would expect, he mentioned how lucky he was to be fully insured because it meant a new car. At other times, if you ask him how he feels, all he can offer is a puzzled look.

These intermediate ego defenses of displacement, intellectualization, reaction formation and repression keep his imperfect survival intact. Men, in particular, are emotion repressors. One of our men got bladder cancer while sharing his situation in a men's circle, a physician sitting next to him told him dark doctor humour, "We say about a person who gets bladder cancer, 'that person is pissed off.'" What makes that so tragic is that anger internalized over many years is suspected of causing cancer.

Vaillant observes basic ego defenses are used to avoid responsibility, control relationships, are enduring, and also tend to piss people off. Imagine how parents can become exasperated with an uncooperative child. The effect when adults use basic ego defenses on each other is even more frustrating. That disconnect is often used as an excuse to use an addiction for temporary relief.

Whereas mid-range ego defenses are also learned in childhood, Vaillant points out they contribute to anxiety, depression, phobias, and compulsive disorders (which include addictions, and assuredly disease).

The way I see it, compared to basic defenses, when people use middle-level defenses they do not frustrate others as much as they signal incongruence. The person's spoken words, tone of voice, and body language often do not fit the context. Others might not be able to quite put their finger on what causes their distrust, but the lack of authenticity is off-putting. This is further isolating.

Countering Strategies

Anxiety exists from mild discomfort to the different animal evident in full blown panic attacks. I have a course called Anxiety Action with 220 slides and several dozen short videos all about it. I am way over my word budget for this chapter but let me leave you with some tips and tricks that may help.

If you called an ambulance for heart trouble or breathing difficulty, seasoned emergency responders will know what is up with monitors and observation. They are likely to have you breathe in and out of a paper bag, which adds carbon dioxide to the blood to compensate for high oxygenation from over breathing, thereby calming your anxiousness.

If you want to create new feelings, you must live new experiences. To change your state, change what you do and what you think. So, first look (focus) to the body and slow your breathing to counter the activation of your lower nervous system under the wolf's feed-fuck-kill-run-hide mandate.

Try doing a body reset: a double inhale through the nose with no exhale in between so that you are intake maxed, then hold, and follow with a long and complete exhale out of the mouth. Do it 2-3 times in a row and you will feel it. I do this reset many times per day; it is better than smoking a joint.

We judge ourselves harshly, others mercilessly, and circumstances unfortunately. Our self-judgment keeps us more than in check, it creates fear, and subdues the spirit. Judging others ensures the belonging we so desperately need is compromised. By judging circumstances as less than ideal, we force ourselves to live in the future, hoping things get better, and fail to see the gift of being alive right now.

Happiness is a decision only found in the present. You can beat any anxiety or panic attack by going for a jog. Reverend Doctor Bruce Pellegrin, an Anglican priest-psychologist at St James parish in Cornwall, Ontario, taught me this one in the late 1980s. Jogging forces your body and brain back into the present.

Compassionate self-forgiveness is one of your best counters to judgment because most judgment occurs within our hearts and minds and without the involvement of others (who usually have no idea). Judgment is an inside job, and so that is where we aim compassion. Take a deep breath and forgive yourself for judging either yourself, others, or circumstances… and let it go. Do this often.

Ask yourself, what connection with whom is under threat right now? Can you refute whatever belief is sustaining your pain? (see appendix B) There is often an old attachment threat surfacing as anxiety.

After reading this, begin to notice when you feel conflicted; this is half the battle. It is OK to feel two ways about something to call attention to a problem. Say to yourself, "I notice I am conflicted, and it makes me feel ___." Inspired by Vaillant's work, choose one of these SARAHS to gather people in.

SARAHS: six advanced ego defenses

1. **S**uppression: in a crisis, you keep it together for everyone's sake, and express emotion later

2. **A**ltruism: The Golden Rule, take the high road using a "best of me" approach (see appendix C)

3. **R**eassurance: I am here, I have your back, we are good. Reassure early in a conflict

4. **A**nticipation: plan and set goals, delay to regroup before reconvening to problem-solve

5. **H**umour: lighten up (appropriately) by not taking oneself too seriously; use self deprecation

6. **S**ublimation: artistic creation, redemption, find the gift or opportunity in every challenge

Your personality might contribute to your tendency to become anxious. Inborn temperament meets environment and forms personality. If you are high in neuroticism, you may carry more negative emotion… but you are unlikely to be the first one eaten by a bear in the woods. Feel better?

Notice that the integrated nervous system denies, distorts, and represses inner and/or outer reality to lessen anxiety and depression. This is the ego in action, part of the default mode network which acts to organize and maintain the being known as you. It's powerful and can alter perception.

When I was a young dope dealer fresh out of high school and living with other teens and runaways in the early 1970s, LSD was a popular drug. The Brotherhood of Brotherly Love out of California were manufacturing high quality stuff and shipping it out according to my suppliers. We did it a lot.

I could pretty much hold it together on psychedelics and was usually the one who babysat others who were having a bad trip or served to reassure those who got really scared doing it.

"Will I always be like this?" someone would say meekly, high as a kite.

"No man, it's just the dope, it will wear off by tomorrow afternoon," I'd respond with conviction.

I can tell you all about bad trips I've witnessed and the dangers of overuse.

There were also times friends of mine did it and it changed their lives. All the miscommunication between them and their parents, the abuse that had gone on, the feelings of rejection and hopelessness, were often replaced with what I called a "cosmic understanding," where the individual, myself included, got a sense of the interconnectivity of all things.

In fact, the views in chapter seven, CHOSEN, were partially derived from recalling those experiences. So, for stubborn trauma, grief, shame, or anxiety, I'm not against trying psychedelics. I can't very well tell you to not do them after having done plenty of them myself. Some people do well on them, but it is hit and miss.

What seems to happen is the ego drops its defensive shield and a new model of the world can slip in and take hold. Though, it quickly goes away unless adopted, and new practices put in place. As a therapeutic tool, it's useful. As a way of life, not so much. I'm not a fan of micro dosing in general.

You cannot escape the need to belong and if you are on psychedelics while others are not, you will soon find yourself out of sync with those around you. This runs counter to how we are made. Since happiness largely derives from a sense of harmony with the people in your world, that must remain the standard.

The problem with anxiety medication is that you never get a chance to experience the discomfort of anxiety and learn more adaptive ways of coping. Watch for that trap. Use breathing, the SARAHS, and check what irrational beliefs have formed (Appendix B). Counter novelty, uncertainty, or powerlessness, by refuting your temporary loss of faith in the future.

Repeat: You can kill any anxiety or panic attack in minutes by going for a jog. This one saved me. Try to control what you can control, closing what Huberman calls the "dopaminergic loop" by creating small wins which might create momentum. Make your bed and clean your room is timeless advice.

Anxiety is no life sentence and as you become wiser, personality changes. You can grow past your misery. Notice how you have invested in an imperfect future, probably like you did as a child, and act to bring yourself back into the present.

Take a deep breath… and let it go.

Summaries

Anxiety is a temporary loss of faith in the future.

Anxiety comes from being conflicted over events, morality, wants, and especially belonging.

Going for a jog at any skill level can alleviate anxiety or panic attacks in short order.

Forgive yourself and others and let go of unhelpful expectations.

Body reset with a double inhale through the nose until maxed and a long slow exhale by mouth, three times.

SARAHS : suppression, altruism, reassurance, anticipation, humour, sublimation.

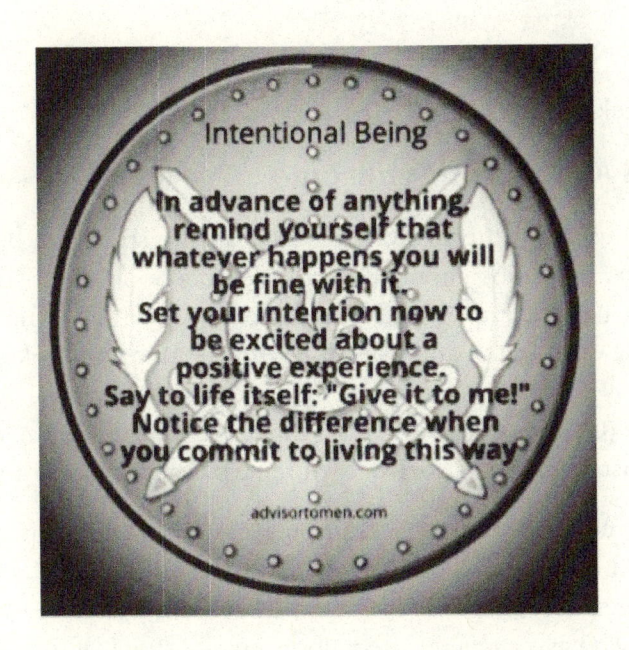

> **Intentional Being**
>
> In advance of anything, remind yourself that whatever happens you will be fine with it. Set your intention now to be excited about a positive experience. Say to life itself: "Give it to me!" Notice the difference when you commit to living this way
>
> advisortomen.com

12. STRESS

In this chapter I'll discuss:

1. General Adaptation Syndrome

2. Nervous System Training

3. Fear Seeker

General Adaptation Syndrome

Addiction uses short term strategies to deal with stress at a high cost to confidence. Any book about addiction is also a book about stress. Hans Selye was a Hungarian Canadian researcher known as "The Father of Stress." He did a ton of autopsies and wrote a bunch of books, including *The Stress of Life* (1956), in which he explains the General Adaptation Syndrome (G.A.S.). G.A.S describes three stress stages: alarm, resistance, and exhaustion (I use GASAREX to remember the whole of it).

Selye realized the alarm reaction "represented the bodily expression of a generalized call to arms of the defensive forces in the organism." He called it "general" adaptation syndrome because "it is produced only by agents which have a general effect upon large portions of the body." And further on he says, "No living organism can be maintained continuously in a state of alarm."

He went on, "If the body is confronted with an agent so damaging that continuous exposure to it is incompatible with life, then death occurs during the alarm state within hours or days."

In the resistance stage, the body adapts to find ways to maintain weight and function, but as the alarm stimulus continues, this pushback is eventually lost. This leads to the third stage.

In exhaustion, Selye notices that the symptoms are like an alarm. "At the end of a life under stress, this was a kind of premature aging due to wear and tear, a sort of second childhood, which in some ways, resembled the first."

Stanford's Andrew Huberman says your adrenals carry two hundred years of stress hormone, so running out is unlikely. It means you can do a lot of damage in the G.A.S. exhaustion stage. Sure enough, Selye writes about how over-stressed animals in his research all eventually experienced catastrophic organ failure of some kind. It also makes me think of the many end-of-life illnesses, such as dementia, Alzheimer's, Parkinson's, and others, in which the body and brain go through a long decline.

The real bitch is that putting yourself into a desire/fear state many times over a long period kills off confidence and brings on learned helplessness, a kind of mental wear-and-tear which, in turn, inches you closer to death. Under any addiction, the catecholamine duo dopamine and adrenaline act to put you in a state akin to doing a brake stand in a car. And, like an auto engine, if you run your body at an elevated RPM long enough, something breaks.

Selye's work suggests that with enough stress, you regress to immaturity, a kind of second childhood he called it. Perhaps unrelated, it is no coincidence that addiction comes with stunted emotions as people run from their stress instead of using it to learn resilience.

Stress can be beneficial, but chronic stress without resolution leaves powerlessness in its wake.

Nervous System Training

Both my parents are dead. One of Dad's regrets was that he would not be able to finish reading all his books, so I am taking a crack at it. One of the salvaged books from their place was clearly Ma's because it is a book about medicine and had a newspaper clipping of a prayer as a bookmark. An unwaveringly devout woman, she was also a trained nurse who once ran a medical office and administered her caregiving to a husband and nine children with a rigorous scientific mind.

The book is entitled *How to Live 365 Days A Year* (1954) by John A. Schindler. He is listed on the inside pages as Chairman, The Department of Medicine, and co-founder at the Monroe Clinic, at Monroe, Wisconsin. The work represents Schindler's observations about human health after twenty years at the clinic, and it is a remarkable piece of work.

Among the many reasons Schindler's book is a prize find is his concept of E.I.I., or Emotionally Induced Illness. The good doctor tells that half the people who arrived at his clinic had no medical reason justifying their presenting symptoms. Physician clients tell me that percentage has gone up.

Schindler talks about tension, stomach pain, headaches, skin problems, and something called muscular rheumatism or fibrositis, all caused by dysregulated emotion. He describes the colon as the "mirror of the mind." This adds truth to the idea that someone can be "a pain in the neck," and a deeper perspective and consequence if they are "a pain in the ass."

Emotionally Induced Illness in Schindler's time is called stress induced illness today.

Neuroception is your unconscious "situational awareness plus prior events" appraisal mechanism. It is your very own "Spidey-sense" intuition about the good, the bad, and the ugly around you. Modulated in the brain mostly by the amygdala, it stays on in everyday circumstances and when we perceive danger.

Mammals have evolved to cope with uncertainty in steps by first connecting and seeking reassurance from each other through the social engagement system. If that fails, things devolve into fight or flight, and then further into immobilization. If you suspect you are by-passing reassurance and heading straight for lower-order nervous-system activation when you get a little stressed, pay particular attention to what follows.

Without a well-developed ventral vagus social engagement (heart, lungs, voice, face), a nervous system trained for protection activates the sympathetic nervous system and fight or flight much sooner than normal or ideal. This narrow tolerance may result in getting pissed off and fighting, or it might mean you fuck off out of there. If you find yourself overreacting in certain contexts, that is a clue.

When you cannot manage stressful challenges by connecting to others for reassurance, and failing that, engaging fight or flight, the dorsal vagus system enacts immobilization. This is when you shut down, freeze, and give in. While it can take various forms, this is your nervous system's white flag of surrender.

At a minimum, it means entering into the infinity loop of the Crazy 8 and a subsequent bouncing back and forth between anger and sadness, frustration, and despair. Procrastination is often described as a form of immobilization borne of perfectionism. Rather than risk rejection from the self or others, a person might find it safer to freeze and do nothing. These also trigger addiction.

Depending on the individual, it can take some time to come down from these episodes. Living this way can also take years off your life, not to mention damaging your relationships and putting happiness out of reach. I'll tell you a bit about my dad in the Appendix as an example.

Chronic stress, from external forces like poverty, war, food insecurity, job loss, accidents, and the like, as well as internal forces like sickness, worry, and addiction, take a toll on body and mind. Stress compounds as it reinforces itself and maintains future stress. All addictions both induce and compound stress as a response to stress. Nuts, eh?

Neurons that wire together, fire together is the essence of neuroplasticity. Overused under stress, the amygdala gets bigger, causing hypervigilance and anxiety. Also, under chronic stress the brain's explicit memory and learning center in the hippocampus gets smaller.

I do not know about you, but I find no comfort in the idea of becoming more nervous and more stupid over time as the result of addiction. Neuroplasticity means what gets repeated gets stronger. To me it means if we do a lot of dumb shit, we get better at doing dumb shit. Am I missing something?

If you do stress, guess what happens? Exactly: more stress, more emotional dysregulation. This has multiplying consequences on every aspect of your being: body, spirit, people, work.

Being easily distracted is one of them. Nir Eyal authored a decent book called *Indistractable* and borrows the acronym HALT (hungry-angry-lonely-tired) to uncover distraction triggers. From the TESTING chapter you know HALT is used in addictions to identify common antecedents.

Since addiction is a coping response to stress, this is a big issue among the population as a whole. You are not addicted to anything but fear, and in my experience, people with chronic stress who report no addictions usually have a secret "functional" addiction of some kind. They just hide it better.

Stress over time will begin to fuck with the immune system's components, especially the cytokine producing microphages. Cytokines exist in a balance of inflammatory (to fight infection) and anti-inflammatory (for recovery). Chronic stress means inflammatory cytokines remain active long after they are needed and activate more quickly in the future. The result is a susceptibility to auto-immune disorders.

Lasting inflammation manifests itself in many ways in the body such as fatigue, fibromyalgia, pain, headaches, arthritis, skin problems, a bad back, asthma, cardiovascular disease, allergies, digestion problems, and insulin resistance. Furthermore, depression, anxiety, schizophrenia,

PTSD, multiple sclerosis, dementia, and even Alzheimer's disease are conditions fed by chronic inflammation of the brain's equivalent of microphages, the microglia.

Not only all that, but inflammation-causing stress from one generation can be passed down to children and their children through the methyl groups, the chemicals which turn on chromosomes. I remember reading how Israeli grandchildren of holocaust camp survivors were adversely affected by methylation generations after the event.

When I solved my riddle of addiction some years ago, my hands were so sore from osteo-arthritis I could barely do a push-up. Holding barbells was painful as fuck, and burpees were out of the question. An elimination diet and careful supplementation got me back on track. No need for me to go on about my 30 years with a sore back. Mindfulness and exercise are part of my daily existence.

Stress responses are about mobilizing energy to meet a perceived threat. That might be something in your environment, or something in your head. Either way you do a quick check to assess if you can manage the stressor while the body and brain coordinate endocrine (HPA axis), immune (inflammatory, non-inflammatory) and autonomic (heart rate, breathing, etc.) functions and spring into action.

Your heart rate goes up to increase blood pressure and pump blood around the body, breathing shallows and becomes more frequent, eyes narrow or widen, focus narrows, the hormone cortisol ensures glucose is released into the blood for muscle movement and thinking, digestion shuts down, skin blood vessels constrict, and blood clotting factors rise in case you are cut. All in a flash.

If you have a history of chronic stress, it is likely that your main stress control centers in the HPA axis (hypothalamus-pituitary-adrenal) are continuing to overdo it. When your nervous system is trained for protection over connection, the speed at which you bypass ventral social engagement and connect to others for mutual reassurance, and instead go right to fight or flight or freeze, is much faster.

You may skip connection entirely. One of my favourite quotes is from Oliver Wendell Holmes Sr.: *"Every now and again a man's mind is stretched by a new idea or sensation, and never shrinks back to it's former dimensions."* So again, now that you know all this, you cannot unknow what you have learned.

Fear Seeker

Since solving the riddle in 2014, at some point I have shown the following Gabor Mate quote to every person I have worked with around addictions: *"For those habituated to high levels of internal stress since early childhood, it is the absence of stress that creates unease, evoking boredom, and a sense of meaninglessness. People may become addicted to their own stress hormones, adrenaline, and cortisol.... To such persons, stress feels desirable, while the absence of stress feels like something to be avoided."* (*When The Body Says No*, 2012)

In my experience, most addicted people are in one way or another fear seekers. They possess a nervous system that arouses easily into fight, flight, or freeze, interspersed with normal functioning. That may be trauma related and it may not; it could be hypervigilance resulting from being in protection mode a lot… and in connection mode not enough. Every ADHD man I have known has this issue: fear addiction.

Whatever the cause, in a wonder of adaptability this unconscious state is what the brain interprets from the nervous system as normal. Remember, most addiction relapses happen when a person experiences success versus failure. Even when things are going well, many of us have a nervous system which unconsciously craves calamity. Now you know where self-sabotage comes from.

At the core of a fear seeker's thinking is a set of maladaptive beliefs about himself of which he is usually not aware. Because the body runs your affective state and situational awareness up to the brain for experience-based interpretation, we want to keep an eye out for faulty beliefs and give them an update or even a delete when they no longer serve us.

Carl Jung taught us that we genuinely want to fix ourselves but are fooled because our eyes see out. This means we end up projecting our internal struggles onto others. If you can get sick under the burden of stress, maybe you can get better by becoming aware of how you think, feel, and act in connection with others as they mirror your internal states. You can if you own it. Remember how the brain works: if you feel something today, you have felt it before.

Since happiness derives largely from what kind of harmony you can create with the people around you, that is a good place to start. It becomes your litmus test for homeostasis. We who are wired for fear simply have to take responsibility and get better at connecting to ourselves and each other from a place of agency and compassion, from a position of power and love.

Your brain uses an accumulation of every thought, action, behaviour, emotional experience, interaction, and environmental influence you have ever had to produce its predictions. You know this now.

As a child growing up in the care of others you lived your environment physically as experiences were encoded in the nervous system. This is especially true in the first decade of life, as a child hears less of what a parent says and more of how it is said.

We have our hunter gatherer ancestors' nervous system. The survival advantages of emotional attunement between parent and child when surrounded by danger in the jungles, forests, or savannahs of our history are obvious.

Experience continued to train the nervous system as you grew, and as your brain got better at abstract thinking, you eventually developed beliefs about yourself that you accepted as fact. If you find yourself addicted as I did, these beliefs are part of the problem. (see CHOSEN, chapter 7 and appendix A)

Shame and its ideas about the self as less than others, or even as broken or defective, is usually part of the chronic stress picture. Instead of seeing the authentic you, others see in you incongruency, where words, facial expression, tone of voice, and body language do not match. That happens because it is what you see in yourself.

In his book *The Placebo Effect,* W. Grant Thompson, M.D. tells of a WWI medic who ran out of morphine and gave water by injection to wounded soldiers. The medic found it worked fine to alleviate the wounded men's suffering until they found out… and then it did not work at all.

He makes the point that it is the therapeutic relationship that accounts for the effectiveness of a placebo. Like with the WWI medic, if you believe in your doctor, it makes sense that your real medicine works even better. Then again, if you distrust your doctor (or your counsellor, shrink, wife, family, friends, or coworkers) you might expect to stay sicker longer. When you have warm relations with people around you, these function as medicine for the soul.

Emotions can cause your illness, but trusting another person makes any help better. Get into an accident or life-threatening dilemma and the difference between suffering or not suffering months or years of PTSD might be in the way someone stands by you in your time of need, holding your hand while reassuring you until help arrives. Medicine for the soul.

What is important to realize is that a nervous system trained one way can learn to operate another way with a little effort and repetition. Before you can do that, you need awareness. It is the autopilot thing again, our ability to use our override system, V.S. Ramachandran's "free won't."

The first thing you must do is log daily times when you felt your nervous system get hijacked by events. This does not have to be complicated, just yes, no, maybe, how, and why. Most people who go from threat quickly, or even straight to responding from the lair of the wolf, are experts in repression. When we repress to the point of not being able to feel, the emotional energy shows up elsewhere, and rarely in an effective or life-enhancing way.

You can sometimes tickle this open in a given situation by taking a deep breath, thinking of energy flowing through the soles of your feet, grounding your being, quieting down a little, and asking "What would I have to believe about myself for this to make sense?" Watch your answer for signs of fight, flight, and freeze. You may be surprised at what you find.

When we do not build improved concepts to meet life's challenges, the predictive brain operates at a deficit on outdated modes of being that include entrenched beliefs. It is like when the operating system on your computer is out of date: it runs slowly... or not at all.

Many of us function on paradigms picked up as kids (which does not mean trauma, though it could). It can be that we have not matured beyond our early years and done an overhaul in preparation for taking full command of life. How about we do that now, claim an identity with which you can live?

Pain is a great teacher, and a certain amount of discomfort helps motivate a man to transcend problems and build competence. When we continue to train our nervous system for protection instead of connection, inevitably there is less energy available for growth and expansion.

The power of placebo is evidence that we can often manage what ails us not just by what we do or how we think, but also by belief, which is especially true when we involve supportive others. It works the opposite way when we feel abandoned by others. Volunteer work, in which you give for nothing, is good practice to get a person back on track.

I often tell people the secret to success is cooperation. Having people in your corner counts. Lisa Feldman Barrett makes the point that if you were planning to jog up a hill, the hill's angle of incline will seem lower if you have a friend beside you, willing to make the run with you.

Elizabeth Stanley in her *Widen the Window* suggests thinking of problems you face and ranking them. Then take one that is not the worst or the easiest. Imagine that issue and how it impacts you, feeling its effects on your nervous system. Rate how problematic it is from zero to ten.

Now think of what would happen in a worst-case scenario, considering the would, could, should, but, if only, and what if of the problem. How much worse does it rate now?

Now turn off autopilot completely and sit in a chair. Take five minutes to imagine the power of the floor supporting your feet and the chair supporting your legs, butt, and torso. Feel your arms being held in your lap or on the armrests. Focus on breathing in and out naturally. Anything you hear around you just allow to go right past you. If and when your thoughts begin to wander, notice it without being harsh on yourself, and just relax and bring your attention back to your body sitting in the chair. Notice the straightness of your back and the posture of your neck and head. Consider your face and ears, eyes, nose, and mouth. Take a deep breath. Now do this exercise from memory.

Chances are the problem's rating dropped gradually as you experienced more here and now.

This could be your future, using mindfulness to check your runaway nervous system and bring you back into the present. I do these kinds of exercises as a matter of course now. It is giving yourself a chance to use your ventral vagus, the heart and mind, to connect with yourself and those around you.

None of us were meant to go it alone. We got "good enough" parents, who had decent intentions and made the best decisions for themselves at the time. If they could have done something differently, they would have, working with whatever nervous system they had from ancestors and caregivers.

This is another opportunity to declare once again "The pain stops here." You can take full responsibility for your nervous system while being aware of your effect on others. This is how you ensure belonging and live your purpose. For it is only by using your power and love in service of yourself and others that you will find meaning and freedom. (I hope that's sinking in by now)

Once again, there is no happiness or even satisfaction possible in the past or the future. Happiness is a decision made only in the present.

Summaries

GASAREX: general adaptation syndrome: alarm, resistance, exhaustion.

Chronic stress with no resolution leaves powerlessness in its wake.

Almost two thirds of doctor visits have no medical reason to support symptoms.

You sought reassurance from others as a child, and this need never leaves (any of us).

We use body, voice, face and eye-gaze to reassure each other.

Watch for signs of fight, flight, and freeze in yourself and those you interact with.

Overused with stress/fear, the amygdala gets bigger and stays on.

Stress/Fear causes thinking and learning to shut down.

Chronic stress makes us more nervous and more stupid.

Distraction is often fight-or-flight.

Procrastination is perfectionism and immobilization.

Stress causes inflammation in the body and brain.

A nervous system trained for protection in childhood often creates a fear seeker in adulthood.

Boredom and restlessness are intolerable to the fear seeker.

Your brain saw you were really scared and survived; you have chased fear ever since.

Fear causes us to take on bullshit beliefs about ourselves.

Ask: What do I have to believe about myself for this to be true?

Having someone to run up a hill with you makes the climb less steep.

Happiness is a decision made only in the present.

Christopher K Wallace

13. LOVE

In this chapter I'll discuss:

1. Oedipal Male

2. Life Cycles

3. Masculine Maturity

Oedipal Male

Once, when my youngest son Howie was five, missus, his sister, the boy, and I were at the supper table. It is the best part of sitting down together as a family to share challenges and victories while reassuring and encouraging each other. Missus told us something she won that day, and I exclaimed, "That's what I like to hear from my woman!" punctuating the air with a little fist pump for enthusiasm.

Sitting to my right, the boy held up his left hand towards me immediately and said, "Wait a minute, Dad…," pausing until he had our attention. "Mommy is MY woman." To his right, his mother sat stunned, an amused twinkle in her eyes. Across the table from Howie, his big sister Charlotte smiled meekly, looking at her brother and then at me, then back at him, and stayed silent.

Charmed, I replied, "Hang on, Son. Mommy is YOUR mom, but she is MY woman."

To which he repeated, shaking his head, "No, Dad, Mommy is MY woman."

From this beginning ensued a couple of years of friendly dad-son ball busting over whose woman the lady of the house was. After all, everyone wants to feel like someone's chosen.

When he was between six and seven years old, from my open office door I could hear him in the living room saying "Mommy, when I grow up, I'm going to marry you."

She answered tenderly, "Oh, Howie, I'm your mom, so I can't marry you, but you will always be my Little Bear," invoking the nickname she gave the boy she bore and has kept alive all these years.

Moments later, "Then I'm going to marry Charlotte," he declared but more as a question than a statement. His mother told him the truth of that one too.

There it was, not even seven, and already the two most important females in his life whom he relied on each day for comfort and direction held no promise of permanence.

And so it begins: confusion at being forced to pull away somehow from basking in the glory of maternal love. Some men, many men, never get passed this masculine hurdle.

Young girls have no such delusions. Despite the tediousness of absurd radical gender theory, little girls know from the outset that they are not growing up to marry Mom.

Some say cultural trends like feminism, the pill, abortion, divorce on demand, and more educated working women have strengthened the other sex and hurt men. Of course, this is mostly nonsense and misses the point. There is nothing in it for nature to make men and women the same. Neither were we designed to be adversaries, but rather we evolved to be complementary. Adding to one automatically should help the other. The problem lies elsewhere.

Not too long ago, Canada celebrated 155 years, and at its confederation in 1867, more than 80% of Canadians would have lived on the equivalent of the family farm. Now it is 20%... or less. I read somewhere that the US family farm is down to just a few percentage points.

When I was a kid in the 60s and 70s, Ma used to tell me to eat my vegetables out of gratitude because of the "starving children in Africa." According to Tufts University professor Alex de Waal, we lost up to 1.4 million souls to starvation per year worldwide up to the year 2000, after which it has been just 40,000 per year, dropping by another third recently in developing countries. That is a 96% or more reduction.

Worldwide, capitalism has been a huge success, lifting billions out of poverty. One of its externalities (unforeseen consequences) is that it commoditizes food and manufacturing production while creating many jobs in cities where people have fewer children. It also takes men out of the home to work, and so there is less masculine influence on young children. This is primarily what weakens males.

Improvements in the plight of women compound the effects of this capitalistic externality, so that now even more kids are raised in single-family homes. The natural contact with men critical to a boy's development has lessened under capitalism's yoke. This has stressed the whole family system.

From a human development viewpoint, I would argue this is also unnatural. Many confused boys grow into men who search for maternal love, a condition Freud called the Oedipal Male.

Life Cycles

That said, in a perfect world, families would be safe spaces where children are not spanked and are held dear with consistency. As resilience researcher Michael Ungar lists in his book, *I Still Love You*, children need parental connection maintained amidst exposure to many other relationships. Kids should be allowed to make mistakes and retain a sense of control, have rights and responsibilities, and form a powerful identity as they trial-and-error their way to maturity.

In the real world, from your miraculous birth, nature hands you off to rank amateurs for safe keeping, no matter what happens. You are reared in the great succorance paradox. Good intentions amidst good enough parenting... which sometimes goes awry.

Professor Randy Thornhill from the University of New Mexico and author of *Parasite Theory* says 100 years ago the #1 killer of children was infectious disease; the #2 reason was infanticide.

A parent's minimal imperative is to keep the child alive. Secondly, it is to socialize a child for two good reasons. One is so that the child's behaviour does not demean the parent's standing among the tribe (Do not bring us shame!). Also, if a child is well-behaved there is a greater chance that members of the tribe will help keep the kid alive. Don't write me letters. Those are just the minimums as I see it.

Many parents do this and much more, while other perfectly imperfect humans with parenting good intentions come up short of ideal. It is a measure of our adaptability that as long as we make it to age twenty and can say please and thank you, nature might consider our upbringing a success. Besides, no one fucks up a kid on purpose. No one ever says, "We're expecting in December, just in time to start creating a disaster child in the New Year." No one.

A child's development follows Piaget's stages of play: sensorimotor (no game), preoperational (game with yourself), concrete operational (game with another or others), formal operational (game with rules, can make rules and new games). If you have children of your own, you will recognize these stages in your kids as well as adulthood's abstract thinking and use of language in yourself.

Erik Erikson took a view that balanced epigenetic and environmental influences on personality over eight stages of life. These are the ones I find most useful.

Those stages include trust vs mistrust in the first year of life; autonomy vs shame and doubt to 2 years; initiative vs guilt from ages 3 to 6; industry vs inferiority from ages 6 to 12; ego-identity vs role confusion in adolescence; intimacy vs isolation in adulthood; generativity vs stagnation from middle age to old age; and ending with ego-integrity vs despair by which you look back in satisfaction or at the horror of impending death.

Most of my work involves Erickson's adult intimacy, generativity, and legacy.

If you had a challenging upbringing, you do not get a do-over with your parents. It also rarely works to forcefully confront parents for their mistakes unless you are in some kind of group therapy together. Otherwise, it tends to make things worse and leave everyone angry. You often need a referee.

If that is not your intent and your folks are alive, you might listen once more to Tony the Restaurateur's advice: "I believe anyone can be walked, it's just a question of approach." Let me tell you how I did it.

When I broached the subject of my father's violence with him in my thirties, he looked conflicted. I could tell he felt guilty, and I realized later he was also protecting my mother. It was she who usually put him up to it, something I could not fathom until after she was gone. My first book, *Drinkers' Riddle*, was written during the months after her death. It kept me busy and allowed me to process my grief.

My folks lived for almost three decades after the day I asked my dad about his violence towards his children. During this time, I took on the task of putting together our family tree. I was inspired to take a different and more indirect tact as a curious genealogist situating my parents in their era.

I asked nothing about me and only about them: the economy, the politicians, the schools, the dances, his first car, his first fight, his relatives, his family, his father, his father's father, the styles, the haircuts, and hobbies. I asked about his first good pair of shoes, his church, his first kiss (he told me about kissing my mother), and the music he liked (he could foxtrot). I asked about the places he had been while he sailed the world for the Canadian Navy. I asked about the jobs he had—he was a cub reporter for the Halifax newspaper before the navy and later chaired the committee that developed the style book for the armed forces and public service...

What you try to do is place your parents in context as much as you can. If they are long gone, sometimes a relative can fill in gaps. By doing so, all the other things you remember about them will make more sense. Like me, you might even come to think, "How could they have behaved any other way?"

If they are alive and you can get them talking, what you also end up doing is honouring them by listening. It is a wonderful gift. If you do not feel they deserve that kind of attention from you, so be it. Read on and you may change your mind. I leave it to you to make the connection to your addictions.

As parents age they revert to a form of childhood while you mature into the adult. The roles change. As you craved acceptance and forgiveness as a child, now you are the parent and can provide those. If your parents could not in their time do so, you get to make things right.

And when either goes, but especially when your father dies, it is you who will step up and talk about your old man because that is what sons do for their fathers. Do the same for your mother. If not you, then who?

Masculine Maturity

More importantly, your responsibility is to remove the idealized version of parents that you entertained as a child and see them for the imperfect souls they are (or were). Armed with this powerful stance, remind yourself to let go by turning "The pain stops here" into a rule.

Refuse to pass along inevitable generational pain to those around you and especially not to your own wife and children. That is one of your life tasks. Assess, keep what is good, ditch the rest.

Women are nature's delegated caregivers and creators of life. You have a small biological part to play in that act of creation, but you have an even greater role as a defender of life. She helps in this regard, but this falls mainly to men. Little boys know this instinctively from a young age and play superhero by five or six. That she creates life and that you defend life is nature's way.

The following is worth knowing, whether you have children and a wife or not, because the odds say that by the time you reach age 49, you will have both.

As a man, you will never know what it is like to spend a year making a baby from your body and delivering life through an opening between your legs. The two years it takes to physically recover from such an ordeal will to you forever remain incomprehensible, as will the need, for better or worse, to instinctively care for a child around-the-clock to adulthood in the way she does.

She has a self-interested brain like anyone else, something she circumvents while using her empathy and compassion to grow the people around her. Her secret fear is that she will be taken for granted, something she feels is akin to enslaved martyrdom. Nobody likes to feel taken for granted, but it is she who creates life, and so her need is greater.

Her shorter ideal fertility period of two decades or so compared to yours at triple that and more, makes her scarce and therefore valuable. So, nature steps in and gives her you: an expendable male.

You can whine about it, or you can accept that this is how things are set up. To me, bitching about nature is futile and immature, and in this case, is a drifting of masculine order over and into the egalitarianism of feminine chaos.

Instead of love, men do better when they honour their need for respect, earned and/or taken, and maintain the loyalty of those whom they defend. To a man, respect is love and love is respect.

That means you earn respect by deeds, by what you do and contribute, by how you defend, deliver, discern and define, discuss and/or delay, and decide—the seven Ds of Masculine Decorum. But first you must defend, especially yourself. That includes taking respect by imposing limits on those who would transgress your sacred mission. Practice and get good at saying no. Respect, earned or taken.

Unlike respect, loyalty cannot be taken and can only be earned. A man must have loyalty around him, or he shall never rest. He is a born defender but needs to sleep at night, knowing others will watch his back while he gathers strength. He also knows that people are only loyal to those whom they respect.

Realize it is only men who can ensure that love prevails in a home, for she cannot do it without you.

In his song "Nevermind" Canadian folk icon Leonard Cohen offers:

"Our law of peace,

Which understands,

A husband leads,

A wife commands."

Men mature emotionally when they stop looking for love; they have reversed the flow. Absent the caregiver's burden, he holds deep reserves of ancestral power and love for those whom he defends in support of meaning and freedom.

Invariably, a man will be loved for this… though he is unconcerned.

Summaries

Every child needs to bask in the glory of their mother's love. Dad too, but especially Mom.

Most little boys at some point want to grow up and marry their mothers. Not so, little girls.

Men are concerned with adult intimacy, generativity, legacy.

You either look back in satisfaction when you are old or forward at the horror of an impending death.

You earn respect by deeds or take it with limits.

Loyalty can only be earned, and people are only loyal to those whom they respect.

If you can't say no, your yes won't mean much, so say no often and yes sometimes.

Men lead, women command.

Only men can ensure love prevails in a home.

Men don't mature emotionally until they stop looking for love; they have reversed the flow.

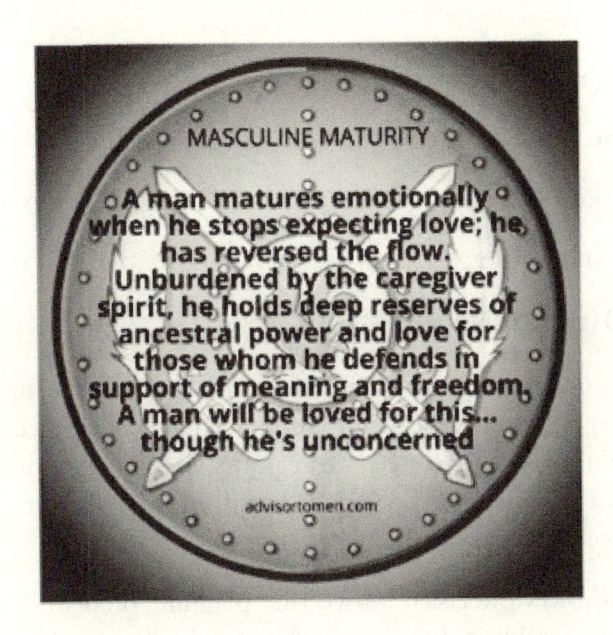

> **MASCULINE MATURITY**
>
> A man matures emotionally when he stops expecting love; he has reversed the flow. Unburdened by the caregiver spirit, he holds deep reserves of ancestral power and love for those whom he defends in support of meaning and freedom. A man will be loved for this... though he's unconcerned
>
> advisortomen.com

14. NEEDS

In this chapter I'll discuss:

1. Six Human Needs

2. Positive and Negative Needs

3. Relationship Needs

The Six Human Needs

Each time anyone engages in an addiction, they are meeting a human need of some kind, albeit not very productively. Nevertheless, an understanding of human needs can point you towards meeting these same needs in a different and more healthful way. That way needs are met, and confidence is kept.

Abraham Maslow once said, "If you are planning on being anything less than you are capable of being, you will probably be unhappy all the days of your life." Understanding your needs and something of the needs of others act as signposts on the road to recovery.

Anyone codifying human needs usually mentions his 1943 work, typically illustrated later on by others as a hierarchy. Physiological needs were at the bottom, followed by safety needs, belongingness needs, esteem needs, and with self-actualization needs at the top.

John Schindler, co-founder of the Monroe Clinic in Wisconsin, says we have six needs: love, security, creative expression, recognition, new experiences, and self-esteem. I understand Tony Robbins adapted these into three complementary pairs to simplify things, calling them The Six Human Needs:

Certainty & Uncertainty, Significance & Love-Connection, Growth & Contribution.

The ranking of needs in importance is context dependent and highly individual. Under The Six Human Needs model, survival requires meeting at a minimum the first four needs, whereas overall life satisfaction requires adaptively meeting all six needs.

How well you can get your needs met influences how attractive you become to others and whether you will be able to form mutually cooperative relationships as opposed to unhealthy dependence.

Adulthood means learning to meet your needs in healthy ways and, if necessary, autonomously.

After all, they are your needs.

We use the word "need" because "desire" suggests something wanted but optional. Stephen Reiss, author of *Who Am I? The 16 Basic Desires that Motivate our Actions and Define Our Personalities*, says desire is a better predictor of human motivation. In his book, Reiss writes about encountering Maslow at a conference and Maslow confiding that he had no idea how to prove his ideas about needs. Needs are also desires, and desires can be about needs; it is just that some needs you cannot do without (the first four).

Driving this point home once more, the whole of your emotional system is based on belonging. When you belong, your emotions rise; when you disconnect, your emotions fall. To that end, polyvagal clinician Deb Dana says, "We are wired for connection, we wish for connection, and we wait for connection."

The risk is that the inability to adaptively meet needs on your own can create despair or unhealthy attachment. Co-dependence between us is normal but exists on a continuum from healthy to dysfunctional. When the individual loses their sense of self, egocentricity may rule their relationships.

Let me explain this further. That a child is egocentric commonly refers to a preoccupation with the self, a "the world revolves around me" sort of thing. The Piagetian view is that egocentricity pertains to speech and thinking directed by individual needs or concerns. You are invited to consider that in a developing brain it also means little emotional separation between the child and parent.

You can imagine again how nature creates "emotional attunement" between adult and child for survival reasons. Imagine again the child crouching near mom in the forest, jungle, or savannah with a threat nearby, the child noticing mom's emotional state, instantly adopting her fear, and staying quiet and hidden.

Emotional attunement is how children experience families physically.

Child psychologist and professor of pediatrics and psychiatry Dr. Richard Tremblay holds the Canada Chair in Child Development and is the 2017 Stockholm Prize winner for his work studying delinquency. He worked with aggressive kids in Montreal schools with little success. He expanded his reach to the families and found that aggressive kids tended to have a mother with issues like depression, anxiety, or addiction. If she only has a female child, the aggression only shows up when that little girl grows up and has a male child of her own. Helping mothers had a positive effect on the children.

Too much attunement can be unhealthy in adults if it means overdependence. Get to know a partner and finish each other's sentences. Become so familiar with each other that you can predict moods and desires, maybe even get good at what makes them happy or sad. But do not lose yourself.

When adult interdependence turns to overdependence, this enmeshment prevents mature love. I prefer words like belonging and attachment on the receiving end in keeping with humans as mammalian herd animals. I like using the word love on the giving end which I'll explain shortly.

Positive vs Negative

Let us look at the six human needs and contrast good and bad ways of meeting needs so you will have rough references for inspiration and guidance. This is by no means an exhaustive list.

Certainty: This is the primary survival need to avoid pain, gain pleasure, and conserve energy. It is the need for safety, stability, comfort, and sustained resources and connections. It supplies predictable order in an often painfully chaotic world.

Positive: creating consistent routines to maintain the body; to nourish soul and spirit; to develop solid work habits that reliably produce sustenance; to form and preserve predictable and stable relationships. It means an internal locus of control, a positive identity, and being organized and orderly while striving for optimism, fortitude, and safety.

Negative: allowing sloth, becoming obsessive or compulsive (including addictions, eating disorders, and cutting), externalizing responsibility, and controlling relationships. It means being unemployed or on assistance beyond necessity, keeping a negative identity, tolerating personal shame, being preoccupied with gloom, self-pity, rape, murder, war.

Variety/ Uncertainty: This is the need for change, challenge, excitement, and stimulus. Paradoxical to the need for certainty, we need various amounts of uncertainty to achieve satisfaction in life by being able to bust out of comfort zones and grow.

Positive: trying new people, places, and things. It may mean traveling, finding new hobbies/passions, engaging in stimulating conversations, networking, meeting people, taking jobs, moving to new areas, watching new plays and films, seeing or doing art, playing games or sports, reading books, or accepting challenges. Life satisfaction, growth and relationships depend on tolerating uncertainty.

Negative: being cavalier, engaging in risky activities without adequate precaution, putting others in danger, in engaging all addictions or self-sabotage, picking fights with significant others when bored or restless, cheating while in monogamous relationships, running away from problems, quitting things on a whim, blaming, creating violence and war.

Significance: Everyone wants to feel like a somebody, to belong, but also stand out and be considered worthwhile and appreciated. Often, this refers to the need for esteem and might also include a spiritual need to manifest our talents and fulfilling purpose. Honour, defined as the esteem of those you care about, bridges significance and connection.

Positive: developing a positive identity, expressing uniqueness, meeting goals, developing style, sharing belief systems that fit a worldview, seeking meaning in life and for existence, allowing oneself to be noticed, putting a hand up in class, accepting compliments, being an analytical person, taking responsibility, rising to challenges, leading others.

Negative: Tearing others down, rescuing people, acting out to get attention, holding a negative identity, engaging in addictions, having a false ego, hiding behind a label, using others to gain status, lying to impress people, denying responsibility, and blaming, raping, murdering, making war.

Love/Connection: This is the need for connection with others and to be part of something. It is the need for belonging, oneness with others, community, and a place in the universe. It is the need to love and, in some cases, to be loved (when young) or at least to belong. Our need for sexual intimacy is in this section, one of the main ways men emotionally regulate with a partner.

Positive: sharing intimacy, being open, joining social organizations, teams, and groups, developing compassion, spending time in nature, seeing the interconnectivity of all things, having healthy sex, enjoying physical affection, exchanging gifts, seeing the good in others and telling them, practicing self-care, giving because you can, spending quality time with others, caring for pets, having a spiritual life.

Negative: Self-sacrificing, joining gangs, having high-risk sex, being sick to gain attention or control relationships, off-loading problems on others, acting helpless, creating bullshit stories about oneself or others, exaggerating sickness or always having problems or becoming accident prone for attention, people pleasing, rescuing others, using addiction to connect to the self or others in unhealthy ways, causing others to feel as if they need us, raping, murdering, making war.

Growth: This is the need to grow and develop, find fulfillment, and self-actualize.

Positive: learning, experiencing paradigm shifts, expanding a model of the world, letting go of old ideals, embracing technology, following bliss, thinking laterally, consulting expertise, accepting advice, honing talents with practice into strengths, seeking wisdom and knowledge, seeing life as a series of lessons, finding meaning in every life event in a continuous expansion of understanding of the self and the nature of existence.

Negative: Pushing too hard, making everything difficult, not finishing things, procrastinating, abandoning unrealistic challenges instead of adjusting, being unable to listen to other people, letting things get to the breaking point before improving them, hyper-achieving, being driven, making war.

Contribution This is the need to contribute beyond your being and to impact your world, the need to give and supply something of value to others, the world, and the universe at large to be effective.

Positive: doing random acts of kindness, being part of things, that one believes in, sharpening talents into strengths and using them to make a difference, helping others because you can, helping to improve one's community, doing one's part and more, giving for the simple joy of giving, focusing on the solution, raising a family, defending others.

Negative: projecting self-centeredness, signaling virtue, using capitalism to rape the planet, joining conspiracies, joining causes that perpetuate problems, having covert contracts, self-sacrificing, making war.

Relationship Needs

Good or bad, all behaviour is need driven. Meeting needs satisfies the self-interested brain. There is plenty of suffering in life, and by meeting needs in a healthy manner, you are more likely to create a life of meaning.

By living a meaningful life, you gain a measure of escape from suffering into freedom.

RMT and Tony Robbins suggest meeting two or more needs by doing something consistently at a five-out-of-ten level or more can become an addiction. That downgrades addiction to habit, and I am not sold on that view alone, while recognizing that the possibility of obsession lies everywhere.

I say addiction is maladaptively ceding control of your being to the body and surroundings in a quest to narrow focus and relieve stress. It is using fear to fight fear. That is beyond RMT's educational agenda, but I bet if we talked we'd soon be discussing nervous systems.

Before allowing circumstances to take over our nervous system and start causing trouble, we could understand the need for trust inherent in the placebo effect and the dangers of the general adaptation syndrome, and contrast these with what needs we are meeting to make sure we remain healthy.

Faced with our addiction, aware of a craving, ask, what need does it meet? Could you meet that need in a more healthful and adaptive way, one which preserves confidence?

Reading over the positive and negative ways to meet needs, you can see the risk is that we bullshit ourselves and negatively meet needs, which eventually create illnesses and a shitty life, slowly heading towards some kind of miserable burnout.

Here I am reminded of Johann Hari's widely viewed video contending the cure to addiction is connection. Besides the risk of relying on Dutton's Rat Park experiments, where I understand replicability was problematic, to me there is a qualification missing. Could we be kinder and more tolerant of addiction around the world? Sure. I am all for the Portugal experiment.

I was also around when Canada's LeDain Commission recommended cannabis legalization in 1972. Then, after I had smoked dope all those years they finally legalized it in 2017. Though I had then figured out the riddle and the cost to my confidence and quit.

So, connection is critical, but it is not a one-way street. I teach men that it is they who need to get better at connecting with others, and not that others need to be more tolerant of their addiction. They are not children who need parenting. They don't have a disease requiring sympathy. They are addicted to fear. The responsibility for their fear habit and for their side of connection is on them. These are their needs, and they must find ways to meet them.

Everyone requires people in their life who believe in them. Maybe you were bullied or even beaten as a kid. Or your dad was at work too often or absent entirely, depriving you of masculine influence. It is time to take full responsibility for your life, happiness, and meeting your needs.

Men compete with each other to determine expertise. We also push each other's buttons from a bit to a lot. Much of this is to check mettle, to test courage.

As mentioned elsewhere, boys know from a young age they are defenders. Rough and tumble play prepares future warriors. Discouraging this is a descent into feminine chaos.

Remember we have the same hunter gatherer brain from before the agricultural revolution. Men and women have always banded together to survive. And men and women can pretty much do anything the other can do in a pinch, outside biology, but with preferences.

If women are the main creators of life, it falls mostly to men to defend life. That will never change.

The other thing is that when two men argue, the threat that one might strike the other if things get carried away keeps things in check between them. That disappears in a group setting when they have allies upon whom they might rely on to fight with them out of loyalty. Because the stakes are higher and broader, men have to be extra careful to not let willfulness get the best of them.

Men also should not allow themselves to be regularly disrespected. Doing so stifles their spirit, and over a long time it risks crushing their soul into learned helplessness. They should start by not disrespecting themselves. It is an act of respect to choose a life of confidence over fear. As I wrote earlier, to a man, respect is love and love is respect. That said, men can usually have intense arguments, even fistfights, and bury the hatchet later without any lingering resentment. The battle is over.

A fella whom I have known for fifty years lives about two miles up the street from me. The first time we met, when I was about twelve, he kicked me in right in the face. We have been friends ever since.

Our happiness is not the only thing that is dependent upon our ability to meet all these needs autonomously. The ability to love powerfully is enhanced by our ability to meet needs in healthy ways all on our own. Addiction negatively meets needs; you can learn to positively meet your needs.

Some might fear that if they meet all their own needs, there will be no purpose for relationships. They might think that means ending up alone and without belonging. The opposite is true.

Instead, reciprocity underpins our interdependence, and we will find that everyone can meet their own needs but also meet some of each other's needs. We only own three things in life: thoughts, feelings, and behaviour. These are always an individual's responsibility. We are responsible to a relationship partner, not for them when it comes to happiness.

For couples, my go-to approach is to recommend Emotions Focused Therapy, developed by attachment expert Dr. Sue Johnson, from Ottawa University. Her books *Hold Me Tight*, and *Love Sense* are both useful. See the online course (Holdmetightonline.com) which I'll link in this chapter's resources.

About half of people have secure attachment styles, and the rest may have developed insecure attachment styles. Insecure anxious and insecure avoidant or a combination of the two occur for many reasons from sensitivity as a child to parental attunement to adversity to environmental influences and even early dating and relationship experiences. Again, the insecure can learn to become secure.

The ego is a tough nut to crack, and some couples need significant pain before they will be motivated enough to start looking after each other's needs. Sometimes a sick child, a move, or an illness, will either break them up or bring them together.

At some point, they may start doing a better job of caring for each other while being clear about how they need their own needs met. Some couples do well with a weekend psychedelic experience though I have no experience with this as a therapy. I mentioned psychedelics in the ANXIETY chapter.

Happiness is easier when you find yourself in harmony with those around you. It is up to you to create conditions that allow you the freedom to love as needed. Born to belong, and for most of us this is our number one need, nothing creates personal expansion more than relationships. No one makes it anywhere on their own. Success requires cooperation.

Going relationship to relationship, trying things out, looking for a sense of completeness, all those encounters inevitably point us back at us. The answer is still the same: that answer is you. You are what you are looking for in other people. It's the eyes-see-out thing again as we project our internal needs onto those around us.

Remember, once you understand projection, you operate from a much deeper wisdom. Being needy in a relationship disappoints because the relationship reflects whatever you lack internally. Rather than solving your problems, the people around you act as tableaus upon which you paint a subconscious life.

You may search for someone to fill a void caused by an unmet need. If you do not fix yourself, these new relationships tend to eventually fall short until you stop and begin to adaptively provide that need for yourself. After all, it is your job to meet your six needs.

From the most enlightened to the consciously impoverished individual, everyone has these same needs. The former is good at the art of meeting needs in healthy ways, while the latter struggles. Choose one.

When needs go unmet, uncertainty and even uncontrollability may rise and leave a gap where addiction can grow. Figure out how you are meeting your needs and/or the needs of your partner. Keep them in mind and discuss meeting needs together. Examine the needs balance between you and others. Replace unhealthy means of meeting the Six Human Needs with more adaptable ones.

When you do this, you will gain power and lose emotional wanting. You will not feel a deficit of the heart. Furthermore, your relationships will be a source of joy instead of pain. Here is how.

The only person in life upon whom you may reliably count on for unconditional love with any certainty is you. This means that when you love others without expectation, you can truly feel love. That includes sexual intimacy. I haven't received sex from missus in 17 years. Getting sex is a weak approach. Be the giver, and the getting will fall into place. Put lust first, and let love take care of itself, because the best way to feel love is on the way out, emanating powerfully from within you. A man's relationships should come from his power as a man and never be his power.

You feel the love you give, and as it passes through your heart and nervous system, through your body and mind to others, you benefit from it first. This is better than any addiction.

Afterall, they say it is better to give than to receive.

Summaries

6 Human needs: certainty & uncertainty; significance & love/connection; growth & contribution.

Meeting needs can be adaptive or maladaptive.

Meeting needs autonomously makes you more attractive as a partner.

Looking to meet needs in others eventually disappoints.

Intimate others reflect back your internal peace or war.

When you love others, you feel the love first.

Conclusion

To conclude I'll discuss:

1. Sex Differences

2. Addiction peculiarities

3. Nervous Capitalism

I am writing from Addison, Texas, which I am told has more restaurants and watering holes per capita than anywhere else in the US. That seems like a good place for a non-drinker to write the ending to a book about addictions.

Contradictions are part of us, not just in single fashion but in their many forms are evidence hinting at the nature of what it is to be human. We are often paradoxical creatures.

We have an internal life but also an external one, each shape shifting one over the other to meet circumstances. We keep certain parts of ourselves secret, often even from ourselves, all the while wearing Jungian masks in contexts around others. We are one way at work, another at home, still another version at church or in the community, and yet another way among men.

Sex Differences

Sex differences also don't get talked about enough either. I think that's a mistake because understanding each other meets many needs, while misunderstanding each other creates confusion and uncertainty that can cue addiction.

The Gurian Institute helps educators see how boys and girls learn differently. It is a favourite subject of mine, and I'll write at length about it later. Here I will just give you some basics. If it opens your mind to sex differences resulting in more tolerance for the other sex, it will have been worth it.

David C. Page, M.D., Professor of Biology at the Massachusetts Institute of Technology, writes, "Our genomes are 99.9% identical from one person to the next as long as the two individuals being compared are two men or two women. But if we compare a woman and a man, the genetic differences are 15 times greater than the genetic differences for two males or two females."

That makes the differences in DNA between men and women at under 2%, which doesn't seem like much until we consider that the DNA differences between humans and chimpanzees is only around 3%.

That last stat usually shuts up the gender confused. Sex and gender matter (terms I use interchangeably, in part as resistance to the idiocy that sees drag queens reading to preschoolers at public libraries).

Geneticist Irene Miguel Aliaga says, "The fact there are differences between the sexes does not mean that one is better and the other is worse." She was recently elevated to the Royal Society of the United Kingdom, of which the likes of Newton, Darwin and Einstein were members, for her research on the gender identity of cells. She can look at a liver cell and tell you if it is male or female.

Men and women have always cooperated. In medieval times there were many European "kingdoms" that were actually run by queens. The two longest serving British monarchs were both women. The Mediterranean during the Bronze Age has seen great queens, notably in Egypt. In short, the record shows there have been plenty of powerful women contributors throughout history.

Writing in *Scientific American* recently, journalist Francine Russo, interviewing Brown University anthropologist Michele Hayeur Smith, quotes her saying, "Textiles and what women made were as critical as hunting, building houses, and power struggles." Russo adds, "In the Viking and medieval eras, women were the basis of the North Atlantic economy, and their clothes allowed people to survive the climate of the North Atlantic."

A gal pal recently sent me a video demonstrating how even baboon males preferred trucks over dolls, whereas the baboon females were solely interested in the dolls researchers left in their vicinity and ignored the trucks. Yet my friend tells me she ignored dolls as a kid, but you should see the incredible gardens she builds every year. Where was she when I used to grow cannabis?

Running sales teams in various cities across Canada for many years, I taught managers how to read maps. Men picked it up quickly, women, not so much. Among my collection of books is *Why Men Don't Listen and Women Can't Read Maps,* by Barbara and Allan Pease. Yet my sister-in-law has the best sense of direction of anyone I have ever known. I sometimes thought that, like birds, she must have magnetic particles in her brain that coordinate with earth's magnetic field, because if I made one wrong turn she would know immediately and point it out.

I contend there is nothing in it for nature to make men and women the same, which holds up as long as we keep things general. In his book *Is There Anything Good About Men?* Roy Baumeister writes about how men and women fill in for each other but have also clear predilections. Just as most women (and men) today lean toward a set of preferences, there are always and have always been outliers.

For example, Baumeister points out that most women tend to keep one or two, usually no more than five, best pals whom they guard jealously from each other and use for emotional regulation. I grew up with four sisters and have found women suffer without trusted friends nearby.

Susan Pinker in *The Sexual Paradox* says the feminine competes by maneuvring covertly, using mean remarks, social exclusion and winning over each other's friends and allies. Some men do this too. In one Israeli study she cites, girls ran against boys and scored best times. Boys ran against boys and scored best times. But when the girls ran against girls their times dropped. Interpret that as you like.

Men tend to operate more superficially while affiliating with many different groups of men around a cause, hopefully something useful. In those circumstances, lest his feelings get in the way, or be used against him, male emotional life is accordingly more reserved. Emotional suppression is our thing.

Baumeister suspects this big group, little group preference is why men seem to be more involved in building cultures. This jives with the durable sex difference that men are about things and women about people. In which case, our preoccupied caregivers stress-test cultures on everyone's behalf

I remember one client who was the only son of a pastor. He'd left home to make his fortune working the oil fields among men who came from far and wide. He was teased mercilessly and sought help. I taught him how men compete among each other to determine expertise but also to test guts. We may ball bust or bully, sometimes cruelly.

In *Warriors and Worriers*, Joyce Benenson says that from a young age males seem to know it will be up to them to defend their community. And so, the selection process begins early as little boys test other little boys to make sure they are not little girls. Again, if you can't take a little teasing now, how will you stand with me later in battle and defend against the enemy? Paradox with a purpose.

Once my client understood how men were competing with him, he could focus on job competence instead while not taking the put-downs so personally. "I am surprised that little girlie car of yours made it here this morning," one burly roughneck might say to him at the start of his shift. He might answer, "Yup, parked it right beside your truck in the ladies section." Bada boom! Admired for his inventive comebacks, he was soon tolerated. It felt good to stand up for himself, and he was fine after that.

My advice is to not get too hung up on "man box" bullshit or the American Psychological Association's "toxic masculinity." Women are just as likely to demand that you "man up" as other men are. In fact, women in general don't get male weakness at all, outside of knowing it exists.

We need to communicate with the opposite sex as partners in Team Human. And just as you are aware of potential violence among men, be aware of how things can go awry with women.

Now put all that into a nervous system context when the two of you are in "discussion." Does she wind up in fight, flight, or flight? Women carry more negative emotion in general and can spot danger faster than most men. Instead of taking it personally, see if you can muster a little sympathy for her adaptive burden, or for what is often generational pain being summoned in survival. When you find compassion for others you also tend to find a little more for yourself. That's how it works.

Let me end this by sharing with you the best advice I have ever received from a woman. My missus taught me this early in our relationship. It fits the egalitarianism sisterhood rule and has withstood the test of time. She told me, "I want people to look at the two of us and wish they were me, not look at the two of us and feel sorry for me that I'm with you." Ouch.

This helped me understand them better than ever. I have taught this simple rule to countless men.

Be mindful of her sensitivity to the "how I believe others see me" part of her self concept. Because she regulates emotionally among peers, it is a prerequisite for surviving, among others.

Sex differences are challenging but also where the most fun can often be had.

Addiction Peculiarities

There are other contradictions about humans. For example, we may hold values which are dear to us, and which support a practical identity that becomes stronger over time. We are also not far from our animal selves, the strictly survival-based wolf, the lower order nervous system concerned only with comfort or discomfort. Its feed-fuck-kill-run-hide instincts can be amplified or muted in environmental contexts and under provocation from each other.

In 95% of us, the left hemisphere is known for language, logic, interpretation, data, and analysis in a closed knowledge system, while the right-side master hemisphere has a broad focus, is an open knowledge system, manages emotion (except anger which regulates in the left), creativity, and intuition.

Generally, the intuitive is imprecise and unreliable; interpretation is as good as the data being considered. If you know a lot about something, intuition may prove true. If not, analyse the data.

A few years ago, I was emailing Roy Baumeister about addictions once more. Unbeknownst to him, I don't think I would have written my first book without his encouragement.

I'd drafted an essay called, "My Epiphany," about a day that changed me forevermore (see Appendix B). I sent the essay to Roy on a whim, (back when I still drank). Roy was sitting in an airport terminal in Germany waiting for a flight and, much to my surprise, read and answered my email in short order.

He said it was important for men in his position to read stuff like what I sent him. Then he corrected my writing like the schoolteacher he was (and is) and challenged me to make it better. Frankly, I was pleased he took the time, and so I did as I was told and rewrote it. I was coming to some conclusions about my drug and alcohol patterns, and Roy's engaging with me gave me just enough encouragement to keep looking. Later, reading his book *Escaping the Self* confirmed I had solved the riddle.

I hope the preceding chapters have helped you see your addiction as a natural response to nervous system arousal over which you had little control only because you were unaware of how it works. Only now you do know, and as I say often, you cannot unlearn what you know.

Having said that, I can fantasize getting ball busted by the likes of Gabor Mate, as in, "You refuse to say addiction is caused by trauma and then have written a book proving it is." So let me qualify and repeat: I just don't see the value in telling every man he has trauma. I prefer the nervous system retraining route.

All of us have made compromises around attachment threats, some worse than others.

How you arrived at being triggered into fight, flight, freeze, or became wired for protection over connection, and used your addiction to cope, is relevant only in so far as it can help you focus on retraining the nervous system to handle specific stressors while caging your wolf to become more.

What's important is to recognize where you avoid emotional closeness and face your resistance.

In my first book, I wrote about how the fear seeker would be first called upon by the chief of the village to go out and scout a new territory or the enemy, or to take up the first watch at night. You need to remind yourself that meeting fear at a different level than others is a gift to be respected. Guard against its downside. You must see that confidence and competence are yours for the taking if you can stop and listen to your body and mind. Your awareness and mindfulness will make the difference.

"Nous avons tous les défauts de nos qualités," say the French. We all have the qualities of our faults and the faults of our qualities. Fear-seeking as burden or gift will depend on how you honour yourself.

Otherwise, the whole trauma bit is not helpful, and I don't see the value. It may even be detrimental.

I emailed Roy Baumeister again a couple years back when I was struggling with the "drug of choice" concept in addictions. Why is it that some people like speed, some like heroin, some like speed and heroin? Others fall for alcohol, some cannabis, some nicotine, the odd person all three. Another might like prescription pills, gambling, overeating, shopping, or porn and, in rare instances, all of those. Roy told me there were so many pathways to addiction that it is probably impossible to figure out.

I've thought more about this since. For example, a relatively high functioning individual of means can use a shopping habit costing tens of thousands of dollars and hide their compulsion behind a façade of success. There are clearly far more functional addicts than known addicts.

I once heard a wealthy man say, "If you can't afford your wife, make more money." All the compulsive shoppers and cosmetic surgery candidates I have known had significant self-acceptance issues and were women, though I did shop compulsively for a time. It was during my woman phase, I suppose.

Gamblers tend to be men, though some women lose fortunes too. I took the RMT training ten years ago based on seeing famed therapist Cloé Madanes narrate a session Tony Robbins did with a mom who had lost money gambling and couldn't forgive herself. The woman had daughters with significant challenges and Tony put two and two together in a masterful intervention.

From my perspective, her gambling was fighting fear with fear and so her guilt served a purpose too. She is a beautiful soul and a dedicated caregiver with whom I interacted a few times later online.

Gambling probably suits men more because of their love of sports and being higher risk-takers. (Note that all-female stock investment clubs tend to be conservative and lose less money) Every once in a while we hear about a bookkeeper or accountant who has embezzled a large sum and blown it all at the casino and faces charges. Wanting is suffering, and opportunity can work against a person. The Addiction Research

Foundation where I studied in the late 1980s noted that, wherever there are more liberal access rules for alcohol, addiction consequences rise. Got to stay off the bike.

A gamer who spends all day at home with his X box or at a gaming café is involved in manufactured excitement and fear with some caveats. If he plays an action game he may build eye-hand coordination and fast reaction time as well as cool under fire, generalizable skills. If he plays fantasy and other such games, which offer no transferable skill building, he may be only satisfying a need to narrow focus.

The hunter-gatherer mind we inherited is less prepared to cope with abundance. Toss in insecure attachment (avoidant or anxious vs secure) and a nervous system trained for protection over connection, and the allure of finding solutions "out there" in wanting is hard to resist.

But now you know. Fear and confidence figure in every addiction. For example, alcohol and fear is well established. Cannabis does the same thing; many casual dope smokers say it makes them paranoid.

A few lines of cocaine make you wide awake, and thinking becomes layered, almost echoing in the mind. Shooting cocaine induces euphoria followed by immediate paranoia, testicles hugging the body, and the penis shrinking like you just jumped into an ice-bath.

Methamphetamine is fear in short order, and both cocaine and meth produce an uncomfortable edge, which can only be relieved temporarily by sniffing, smoking, or shooting more.

All the addictions activate the lower-order nervous system, the feed-fuck-kill-run-hide of the wolf. The peripheral nervous system involved in fight or flight activates most obviously with psychoactive substances but also with gambling, gaming, and even sex addictions and porn fairly clearly.

The dorsal vagus is sub-diaphragmatic, influences digestion and sexual function, and factors in the immobilization of the freeze effect. Porn both excites and brings on fear as the porn user worries about being caught in his compromised position (What if I'm hacked?). He also experiences a parasympathetic refractory period post-orgasm that meets a need for immobilization. The absence of a real partner kills desire under habituation. More confidence down the drain, so to speak.

Again, the dorsal vagus figures in over-eating, by which, in order to relieve stress, the eater puts themselves from mildly "stuffed" all the way to "food coma" and more immobilization. Food definitely immobilizes, and bingeing and purging is fight-and/or-flight-and/or freeze. Where is confidence then?

The overeater also uses fight or flight when they beat themselves up for a time about their lack of willpower: "My belly is so fat, I'll never get laid! I haven't seen my dick in two years!" That self-recrimination is part of his fight-or-flight escape. Remaining focused on how fat, repulsive, and undisciplined he is, he avoids life's problems with a "safe" problem. It's fighting fire with fire.

Many more men than ever before have porn addictions. Some start as young as eight or ten years old, soon after their parents gave them their first phone. I hear from men who, as high school kids going to prom with a dream date, were not able to get an erection despite a willing partner.

I see men in their thirties who have been into porn two decades and who want to date the pretty girl signaling him at the office every day. He knows full well that if he went home with her and attempted sex, he would face the almost certain embarrassment of ED. Imagine the effect on confidence.

I see middle aged, addicted men with learned helplessness who have now totally given up on partner sex and intimacy. All of these conditions are reversible.

Where the drug of choice porn equivalent comes in is that beginner users will watch amateur uploaded porn and slowly experiment. At some point, the experienced porn user will develop what we call a "kink," a preference of one genre over another. It becomes their go-to get-off you could say.

What makes me think of my conversation with Roy is that I've heard the back story from men addicted to porn who have developed a kink. I know their childhoods. I find their kink is related to some aspect of their upbringing or history. That doesn't mean it is trauma, for fuck's sake. It means if I listen long enough I can usually connect the kink and an earlier influence. You do what you know.

One man who grew up with a deeply unhappy mother beset with anxiety and depression, on a variety of meds, and in and out of care, found in adulthood he gravitated towards gang bang, or multiple actors pleasuring one woman. Think it's related? I think it is.

A white man from a deeply religious and segregated order with an intolerance of outsiders, who found himself as a boy under the influence of a judgmental, outspoken, bigoted and even racist mother, now finds himself hopelessly addicted to watching big booty Black women. Think that's connected?

There are many such examples. If a man is addicted to porn and comes to understand the source of his kink influence, the allure leaves them more or less permanently. It's difficult to enjoy gang bang porn when you realize the woman actor is a stand-in for your mother. Again, once a man understands his projections, he operates from a much deeper wisdom.

Regarding cannabis use, upon hearing my theory around solving the riddle of addiction, my son called me a buzzkill. I took it as a compliment. I aim to do the same for porn users, not because I'm totally against porn but because of its potential for abuse. Kill the buzz, gain the confidence…

Nervous Capitalism

According to Hans Rosling in *Factfulness*, in the year 1800 some 85% of the world lived a level-one existence. That's the equivalent of one dollar per day, being barefoot mostly, and walking for water from a hole in the ground. It means gathering wood for fire, always eating pretty much the same thing, and a crop failure results in starvation. Sickness usually leads to death, especially for kids, making average life expectancy around 30.

By 2017, 6 of 7 billion people around the world live above the 1800 standard, and life expectancy is 72.

You have already read about how world starvation went from roughly a million and a half souls per year prior to the year 2000 and now sits at a few tens of thousands, depending on who is at war with whom.

The point is that capitalism is a wonderful system to grow economies and personal wealth and, especially, innovation. The simplified problem is two-fold. One is growth. Capitalism under the fiat money system requires two or more percent expansion each year. That has an effect.

Arguably, an even greater effect is how capitalism now rules every facet of our existence. Like I said, at confederation more than 80% of Canadians lived on the equivalent of the family farm. They had men around them to mentor them for good or for bad. They had the apprentice system.

Since the rise of the middle class during the Victorian era, privacy has become a thing, and most men work away from their wives and children a good part of the day. This leaves boys reliant upon maternal forces for far too long. We have grown our economies but not our boys. Warren Farrell says it is a boy crisis in a book of the same name: the west full of weakened men under capitalism.

Feminism and the rise of women power in societies has occurred in a vacuum of male weakness. Now women face the same thing, only it is often without a man by her side to help her manage. Birthrates have plummeted. That's not how nature intended things. I will turn my attention to this in 2023.

Mary Eberstadt writes about this general cultural upheaval in in her 2019 book *Primal Screams*. She provides a ton of sources, including Harvard's Carle E. Zimmerman's study *Family and Civilization*, in which he cites high divorce rates, declining fertility, mainstreaming sexual diversity, and that "positive social antagonism to the old domestic family system and the family among the whole masses of people" as factors present at the fall of Roman civilization.

Considering the fall of the Romans is framed as the fall of western civilization, we should listen up. When it happened, people forgot how to read, write, build stuff, and be mothers and fathers. We want to be incredibly careful going forward, and the next hundred years will be critical.

Look, fuck Marxism, but I think the sisterhood needs the brotherhood to figure out how to get out from under the yoke of capitalism's excesses for the sake of Team Human. We need capitalism to work for us, not just see all of us working blindly to support capitalism. We first change what we can, ourselves.

In summary, the world desperately needs powerful men. I am hoping you will be one of them.

The purpose of this book has been to show you the fear-over-confidence continuum in addictions. A secondary aim has been to make you acutely aware that how you think, feel, and behave is all your responsibility because what you feel today, you have felt before. Anytime you are out of sorts, there is a connection to your past in there somewhere that you can learn to decipher. To feel differently, you must live differently, with 100% responsibility for your thoughts, feelings, and behaviour.

I realized happiness is a decision in the mid-1980s while reading Norman Vincent Peale, and it changed my life. It is my hope you will arrive at a similar awakening around fear addictions and confidence.

As children, we receive most of our guidance through the positive and negative regard of others. As adult men, this largely reverses as we accept our talent with humility and responsibility. By now, you know the drill: a man who uses his power and love in service of himself and others finds meaning and freedom. Power and love are two sides of the same coin; force is something else.

Your combined body and mind, your being, is a highly adaptable but incredibly sensitive organism that deserves your best care. Maintenance of the body is first. I wear the Oura ring to track my sleep, heart rate, and heart rate variability, recording my workouts as I go, but there are many ways to do that. Paper and pencil tracking will do in a pinch.

Without being obsessive, I monitor food and water intake and exercise once or twice per day. Doing Andy Frisella's "75 Hard" should be on your list to kickstart the body if your health allows it. I am just a little guy and almost 65 but still push the 75-pound dumbbells and do sets of 80 fast push-ups (100 if Missus is counting). Instead of polluting your mind and body, become scientific about its maintenance.

Stick around: I invite you to live to one hundred with me.

If you are not meditating, I'd recommend at least doing one- or two-minute time outs every hour. The double inhale though the nose and long slow exhale through the mouth done three times is my go-to body reset. I dabble in the breath exercises found in the appendix of James Nestor's book *Breath*. I also like Elizabeth Stanley's *MMFT* because she is top notch and comes from a warrior background herself. Your last breath was pretty important but not as critical as your next one. Make it good.

I also walk the land on a track I keep mowed in summer and snow-blown in winter. If I'm not tossing the 20 lb ball, I breathe in for a count of six and out for a count of six while Glide-walking, something I learned from Esther Gokhale in *8 Steps to a Pain-Free Back*. Firas Zahabi's *Strong and Stable Back for Life* saved me when I'd recently overdone it on the leg press and had to use two canes for five days. The Alexander technique he demonstrates stopped the spasms.

I like Hyperbolic Stretching with Alec Larsson when my back is cooperating. I'm a big fan of the guys at Gold Medal Bodies (GMB) and do their starter floor stretches almost daily. I am in the midst of doing "75 Hard," and I've been able to mix it up with a little cardio, weights, and body-weight training.

Consult an expert for help with diet and supplements. For microbiome and healing I like the hydrogen tablets from drinkhrw.com. I blew both shoulders, one after the other, some years ago and fixed one at the hospital followed by a bunch of rehab and the second one in a few weeks on high doses of hydrogen water. I also like that the CEO runs scientific trials with his products. I also take their Ageless Defense, and their Build creatine product. I'm a three liters of water per day type.

You might have a place you call home, but the body is the universal address of your existence.

Some of you are good sportsman, which is great if it is active (poker is not active). Watch for obsession, though, and when spotted, call out your nervous system and use a body reset. I also like Shirzad Chamine's *Positive Intelligence* for its simplicity and accessibility. Get your saboteurs and positive intelligence scores for free at his site. One of his first trained coaches, I use it daily with men.

Everyone should learn self-hypnosis for sleep, napping, and settling themselves down for things like flying, public speaking, exams, and important meetings. You can whet your appetite with my free napping course below. Three decades ago, I cured persistent insomnia with three months' nightly practice. There's a longer Cure Your Insomnia course containing my favourite methods too.

Lastly, a man must claim an identity and live according to values he's carefully chosen to assist him in his purposeful pursuit of mission. Every man needs this, regardless of disposition or mix of talents. Any craving is a calling from your spirit to live powerfully.

You were chosen for life by the heavens, and they don't make mistakes. You have something to contribute, so don't fucking hold out on us.

Who would you need to be to honour the life you were given (in ways small and large)?

And next time you hear someone talking about how an addicted person has to "hit bottom" and "decide for themselves" and that there is "nothing you can do," you will have the courage to call bullshit. You can tell them they are not at all addicted to whatever has their attention. Rather, they are simply addicted to fear. Spread the word, plant the idea, so truth displaces fear and confidence grows

Set an example by choosing confidence over fear yourself. We need you. Use your power and love in service of yourself and others to find meaning and freedom. That is how you make your life count.

What else is there in life but making a difference?

Christopher K Wallace
Addison, Texas, USA,
Oct 2022

Summaries

Male and female DNA differences are under 2%; between chimps and humans, 3%.

Men and women naturally band together to take advantage of strengths and shore up weaknesses.

Men compete head-to-head to determine expertise and test mettle by ball busting and bullying.

Women maneuver covertly using mean remarks, social exclusion, and winning over each other's allies.

The rise of feminism and female power has occurred in a vacuum of male weakness.

Capitalism has grown the living standard of the world but cost boys male influence at home.

The world desperately needs powerful men.

You might have a place you call home, but the body is the universal address of your existence.

Use your power and love in service of yourself and others to find meaning and freedom.

What else is there in life but making a difference?

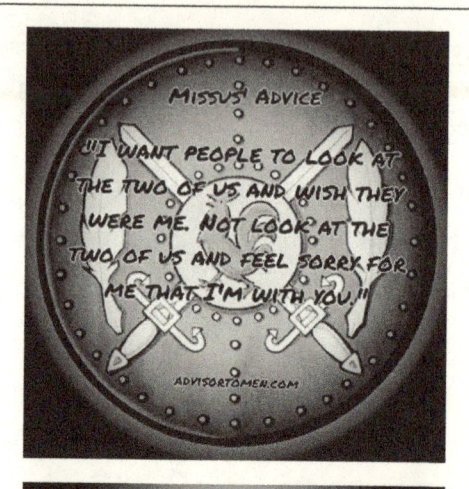

Missus' Advice

"I want people to look at the two of us and wish they were me. Not look at the two of us and feel sorry for me that I'm with you."

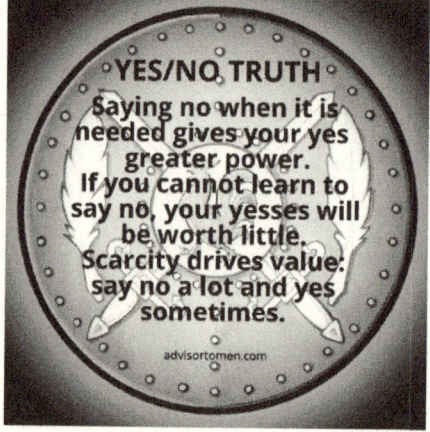

YES/NO TRUTH

Saying no when it is needed gives your yes greater power. If you cannot learn to say no, your yesses will be worth little. Scarcity drives value: say no a lot and yes sometimes.

RESOURCES

1. Crux

Shelley Taylor, *Tend and Befriend*, 2000

Spencer and Hutchinson, *Alcohol, Aging, and the Stress Response*, 1999

Mark Huberman, Huberman Lab podcast #86

https://hubermanlab.com/what--alcohol-does-to-your-body-brain-health/

Eric Burden and War, "Spill the Wine," 1970

Roy Baumeister, *Escaping the Self*, 1991

Brian Hayden at Simon Fraser and his colleagues on brewing way back

Hayden, B., Canuel, N. & Shanse, J. What Was Brewing in the Natufian? An Archaeological Assessment of Brewing Technology in the Epipaleolithic. J Archaeol Method Theory 20, 102–150 (2013).

Nako Nakatsuka and Anne M. Andrews, *Differentiating Siblings: The Case of Dopamine and Norepinephrine*
https://pubs.acs.org/doi/pdf/10.1021/acschemneuro.7b00056

Cleveland Clinic: *Epinephrine (Adrenaline)* Basic explanation of adrenaline and epinephrine

https://my.clevelandclinic.org/health/articles/22611-epinephrine-adrenaline

Yadollah Ranjibar-Slamloo, Zeinab Fazlali *Dopamine and Noradrenaline in the Brain; Overlapping or Dissociate Functions?*

https://www.frontiersin.org/articles/10.3389/fnmol.2019.00334/full

Kent Berridge, *Delight, Desire, and Dread: Generators in the Brain* (I found Kent's work after writing Drinker's Riddle in 2015, and while his studies were on rodents, the ideas support my fear/desire contentions, especially the way addiction narrows focus)

https://youtu.be/hrf8FlVoR_I

2. Confidence

Gyorgy Buzsaki, *The Inside Out Brain*, 2021

Rosabeth Moss Kanter, *Confidence*, 2006

Kent Sayre, *Unstoppable Confidence*, 2008

Martin Seligman, *Flourish*, 2012 (Seligman gave us the concept of Learned Helpless)

3. Wanting

Arthur Schopenhauer, *The World as Will and Representation*, 1818

Marge Loughlin, for pie @Loughlin's Country Store, Hallville, Ontario

C. K. Wallace, *Drinkers' Riddle*, 2015

Graphic: *"Fighting Fire with Fire"* (water versus flamethrower

4. Winning

Mike Gazzaniga, *The Social Brain*, 1985, and *Who's in Charge?*, 2011

Daniel Lieberman, Michael Long, *The Molecule of More*, 2018

Anna Lembke, *Dopamine Nation*, 2021

Robert Glover, *No More Mr. Nice Guy*, 2001

Viktor Frankl, *Man's Search for Meaning*, 1946

William Ernest Henley, "Invictus," 1875

Keith Richards, Mick Jagger, "You Can't Always Get What You Want," 1969

Jordan Peterson podcast episode #296 with Mark Huberman

https://youtu.be/z-mJEZbHFLs

5. Testing

Ann Graybiel, Kyle Smith, "How the Brain Makes and Breaks Habits," Scientific American, 2014

https://www.scientificamerican.com/article/how-the-brain-makes-and-breaks-habits/

Roy Baumeister, *Escaping the Self*, 1991

Andy Frisella, "*75 Hard*," https://andyfrisella.com/pages/75hard-info

6. Caging

György Buzsáki, *The Brain from Inside Out*, 2019

Deb Dana, *Polyvagal Exercises for Safety and Connection*, 2022

Stephen Porges, *Polyvagal Theory*, 2011

Lisa Feldman Barratt, *How Emotions Are Made*, 2017

Glenn Livingston, *Never Binge Again*, 2015

Graphic, "3-2-1+ Nervous System" based on Deb Dana and Stephen Porges's Polyvagal Theory

7. Chosen

Viktor Frankl, *Man's Search for Meaning*, 1946

Lisa Feldman Barratt, *How Emotions Are Made*, 2017

Steve Chandler, author of 40 books, all good ones

Joseph Campbell, *Pathways to Bliss*, 2004

Mihaly Csikszentmihalyi, *Flow*, 1990

8. Trauma

Glenn Livingston, *Never Binge Again*, 2015

Paul Bloom, *Just Babies*, 2013

Roy Baumeister, John Tierney, *The Power of Bad*, 2019

Gabor Mate, all of his work is good, I'm still reading *Myth of Normal*, 2022

Michael Ungar, *Change the World*, 2019

Timothy Wilson, *Redirect*, 2011

Roy Baumeister, John Tierney, *Willpower*, 2011

Jeffrey Young, *Reinventing Your Life*, 1994

Habib Davanloo, *Short-Term Psycho Dynamic Therapy*, 1992

Patricia C. Dell Selva, *Intensive Short-Term Dynamic Psychotherapy*, 1996

Peter Levine, *In An Unspoken Voice*, 2010

Donald Epstein, *The 12 Stages of Healing (a network approach to healing)*, 1994

Bessel van der Kolk, *The Body Keeps the Score*, 2014

Stanley Rosenberg, *Accessing the Healing Power of the Vagus Nerve*, 2017

Deb Dana, *Polyvagal Exercises for Safety and Comfort*, 2020

Judith Blackstone, *Trauma and the Unbound Body*, 2018

The Integration Courses, Taming Shame, (every man should do this one)
https://services.advisortomen.com/courses/taming-shame

9. Emotions

Lisa Feldman Barrett, *How Emotions Are Made*, 2017

Robbins Madanes Training, "The Crazy 8"

Phil Stutz, Barry Michaels, *The Tools*, 2012 (contains Active Love, similar to Universal Love)

Moore & Gillette, *King, Warrior, Magician, Lover*, 1990

Jordan Peterson podcast episode #296 Andrew Huberman

https://youtu.be/z-mJEZbHFLs

10. Depression

Christopher K Wallace, Depression, advisortomen.com, 2019

Steven Barnes, *Lifewriting*

https://podcasts.apple.com/us/podcast/lifewriting-write-for-your-life

Joseph Campbell, *The Hero with a Thousand Faces*. 1949

Douglas Hofstadter, *I Am a Strange Loop*, 2007

Robert Glover, *No More Mr. Nice Guy*, 2000

Martin Seligman, *Flourish*, 2012

11. Anxiety

Paul Bloom, *Just Babies: The Origins of Good and Evil*, 2013

Roy Baumeister, Mark Leary, *The Need to Belong, meta-analysis*, 1995

George Vaillant, *The Wisdom of the Ego*, 1993

George Vaillant, *Ego Mechanisms of Defense*, 1992

George Vaillant, *Triumphs of Experience*, 2012

Anna Freud, *The Ego and the Mechanisms of Defense*, 1966

Amy Hardison, Alan Thompson, *The Ultimate Coach*, 2021

Michael Pollen, *How to Change Your Mind*, 2018

Christopher K Wallace, "Anxiety Action" course here:

https://services.advisortomen.com/courses/anxiety-action

Jordan Peterson podcast #296, *Neuroscience meets psychology*, Andrew Huberman

https://youtu.be/z-mJEZbHFLs

12. Stress

Hans Selye, *The Stress of Life*, 1956

John Schindler, *How to Live 365 Days a Year*, 1954

W. Grant Thompson, *The Placebo Effect*, 2005

Gabor Mate, *When the Body Says No*, 2012

Shirzad Chamine, *Positive Intelligence*, 2016

Elizabeth Stanley, *Widen the Window*, 2019

(see her MMFT program online)

https://www.soundstrue.com/products/mindfulness-based-mind-fitness-training

See the Israeli descendants' methylation discussion here

https://www.scientificamerican.com/article/descendants-of-holocaust-survivors-have-altered-stress-hormones/

13. Love

Sigmund Freud, *The Interpretation of Dreams*, (first mentions the Oedipus Complex)

Herbert Ginsburg, Sylvia Opper, *Piaget's Theory of Intellectual Development*, 1969

Erik Erickson, *Childhood and Society*, 1950

Randy Thornhill on the Jordan Peterson podcast, 2021

The Caregiver Archetype is from the works of Carl Jung

https://www.un.org/esa/socdev/family/docs/men-in-families.pdf

Alex de Waal, *Mass Starvation: The History and Future of Famine*, 2017

Census info from the period in question here:

https://www12.statcan.gc.ca/census-recensement/2011/as-sa/98-310-x/98-310-x2011003_2-eng.cfm

Warren Farrell, *The Boy Crisis*, 2018

Leonard Cohen, "Nevermind," 2005

Robert Glover, *No More Mr. Nice Guy*, 2000

Dr. Randy Thornhill, "Death, Disease, and Politics," The Jordan B. Peterson Podcast

14. Needs

A.H. Maslow, *A Theory of Human Motivation*, 1943,

http://psychclassics.yorku.ca/Maslow/motivation.htm

Stephen Reiss, *Who Am I? 16 Basic Desires that Motivate Our Actions and Define Our Personalities*, 2002

John Schindler, *How to Live 365 Days a Year*, 1954

Magali and Mark Peysha, *Strategic Intervention Handbook*, 2014

Roy Baumeister, *Is There Anything Good About Men?*, 2010

Sue Johnson, *Hold Me Tight*, 2008, *Love Sense*, 2009

Find Hold Me Tight online here:

https://holdmetightonline.com/

Conclusion

Hans Rosling, *Factfulness*, 2018 (this will give you the facts about the world)

Joyce Benenson, *Warriors and Worriers*, 2014

Susan Pinker, *The Sexual Paradox*, 2009

Mary Eberstadt, *Primal Screams*, 2019

Carle E. Zimmerman, *Family and Civilization*, 1940

Elizabeth Stanley, *Sounds True*, MMFT

https://www.soundstrue.com/products/mindfulness-based-mind-fitness-training

Christopher K Wallace, "Taming Shame" course here

https://services.advisortomen.com/courses/taming-shame

Andy Frisella's "75 Hard" program here

https://andyfrisella.com/pages/75hard-info

The Gurian Institute here (I lifted Page's quote from one of their articles)

https://gurianinstitute.com/

Esther Gokhale, *8 Steps to a Pain-Free Back*, 2008 (really helpful)

Firas Zahabi, *Strong & Stable Back for Life*, on YouTube and at https://strongandstable4life.com/

James Nestor, *Breath*, 2020

Gold Medal Bodies, on YouTube and at https://gmb.io/

Alec Larsson, *Hyperbolic Stretching*, https://hyperbolic-stretching.com/

Alex Tarnava, Drink HRW blog, at https://shop.drinkhrw.ca/

Christopher K Wallace, "The Napping Advantage" free course at

https://services.advisortomen.com/courses/the-napping-advantage-your-self-care-secret-weapon

Sign up for my newsletter @

http://www.advisortomen.com

©CHRISTOPHER K WALLACE, 2022, Sipping Fear, all rights reserved advisortomen.com

APPENDIX A

Irrational Belief reframes (Based on the work of Albert Ellis)

Asking yourself, "what do I have to believe to make this true?" and listening for your truest answer often lets you know that an irrational belief was somehow installed in your mind at some point.

Notice how this errant belief affects your thoughts, feelings, and behaviour. Now, rebuild that belief into something which helps instead of hinders your existence. Be free of it.

Here are some common ones along with some counters below to get you started. Add in any of your own and reframe them.

Go down the list on the left. Which ones apply to you a bit or a lot. Refute them, they are all bullshit.

Replace the irrational belief with a more reasonable one, similar to how I riffed them on the right.

Simplified versions of irrational Beliefs

I believe…

1. I must be liked or even loved by everyone	1. Not everyone will love or even like me
2. I must be successful, or I won't be liked	2. Your belonging is not contingent on success

3. People must treat me fairly
4. It's bad when plans change
5. I can't help how I feel
6. Worrying keeps me safe
7. It's better to avoid problems
8. I can't get by on my own
9. You cannot get away from your past
10. I can't help being affected by other's problems
11. There is always one right way to proceed
12. I need everyone I know to approve of me
13. I must avoid being disliked from any source
14. To be a valuable person, I must be good at everything I do
15. It is not OK for me to make mistakes. If I do, I am bad
16. People ought to make sure I'm happy
17. People who don't make me happy deserved to be punished
18. Things must work out the way I want
19. My emotions are ills I am powerless to control
20. I cannot feel happy in life without contributing in some way

3. No one owes you anything
4. Change is part of life
5. We own our thoughts, feelings and behaviours, everything else is transient
6. Worrying is misplaced imagination
7. Avoiding problems tends to make them grow
8. I am capable
9. The past does not define your future
10. I am not responsible for other's problems
11. There are as many options as we can imagine
12. I realize not everyone will approve of me, that's **OK**
13. If someone dislikes me that is on them
14. "Nobody knows the all of anything." (Robertson Davies)
15. Mistakes are how we learn, and we all make them
16. Others are not responsible for my happiness
17. My happiness is my business
18. The universe doesn't revolve around me
19. My emotions are my responsibility
20. I am happy to contribute each day in some way

21. Everyone needs to rely on someone stronger than themselves	21. I work well with others, or I can work fine alone
22. Events in my past are the root of my attitude and behaviour today	22. Each day I get to create a new me if I choose to
23. My future outcomes will be the same as my past outcomes	23. My past outcomes taught me how to be better
24. I shouldn't have to feel sadness, discomfort, or pain	24. Suffering is part of life and pain teaches
25. Someone, somewhere, should take responsibility for me	25. I alone am ultimately responsible for me

You could say, "I used to belief x but now I believe y."

Next time you feel anxious (or negative) look over the list to see which one might be sustaining your discomfort and refute it to restore your mental fitness. See how much more powerful you feel.

Find and fix your thinking. Reframing old beliefs which no longer serve you or those around you gives you freedom. Ask: Does this still work?

Sustain freedom by using your personal override system, your "free won't," to create new feelings by living new experiences. Soon your brain will be retrained with new concepts to use in the future.

Repetition as the mother of learning works best with emotion.

Change your state, change your life.

* From The Anxiety Action course. Find it here:

https://services.advisortomen.com/courses/anxiety-action

APPENDIX B

This appendix contains a dozen anecdotes given as background to some of the ideas and characters from inside the main pages of the book.

MA

My mother hailed from a family of nine children born to a whiskey salesman and stout Newfoundlander mother. She was given to her mother's mother soon after birth, her mom supposedly saying to her mother, "I just couldn't bear another one." So, she was reared in a house with her grandmother nearby. All that time, her siblings were together, she alone with Grandma. At fifteen, she was allowed to stay overnight at her parents' home. The next morning, she refused to leave. She married my dad, a naval officer, who was gone for weeks and months at time. He'd been advised by an old colonel to keep her "barefoot and pregnant" to manage the long absences. Ten pregnancies in twelve years resulted in nine children of her own. Clearly, Catholics. She lost one before me in the mid-50s, blaming it on painting the basement stairs with lead paint in the third trimester. Trained as a nurse, she had a keen scientific mind. She raised her children and tended to my father in early retirement. She developed osteo-arthritis in her hands (like I have) in middle age and spent decades pushing through her pain to knit hats and mittens for the poor on behalf of her church. In the last few years of her life, she first got bladder cancer, underwent treatment, and saw it return in the liver stage four. She died after a two-day vigil in her living room, surrounded by her nine adult children. Her husband of sixty-two years, whispered sweet reassurances and thanks as she went. She was carried out "feet first" as promised. Rest in peace, True and Free.

CONFIDENCE TRICK

The day before, the kids were at a travelling fair set up in the casino parking lot not too far away. On that first visit, Charlie passed on some of the scarier rides. So did Howie. Finally, missus resorted to bribery. "I'll give you five bucks if you go on this one…" she declared. Later, I told Howie I'd seen pictures of him on the rides and couldn't believe he was on them alone. He told me that the pirate ship is pretty hard on a boy's balls when it swings high in the air. I wasn't sure I'd heard right.

"Dad, it crushes my privates." We all laughed together in sympathy.

"But you were brave enough to go on it," I said, "even by yourself. I'm impressed!"

He replied, "I know a secret about courage when it comes to rides like this."

"Oh, really, a secret about courage? Let me hear it."

Howie smiled, looked off in the distance a little and replied soberly, "I figured out you only need enough courage to get in the seat of the ride. After that you can be as afraid as you like."

From Howie, a confidence trick worth remembering.

THE 90/10 RULE

In 2017 Northwestern University did a study about studies, reviewing 17 million pieces of research while seeking to discover how much new information versus already known information they contained. The findings were that 90% of your average study contains old knowledge. The worth of the study was in the remaining 10% of new information which advanced things. Similarly, you and I are comprised of the people around us. We are eclectic amassers of bits and pieces from here and there over years that become you. Chosen by heavens of infinite wisdom for life, there has never been another one of you and there will never be another again. You are irreplicable. You have something unique to bring forward for the benefit of all of us. Don't seek first to re-invent the wheel; practice making the wheel better. One small tweak, a new way of looking at things, lateral "outside the box" thinking with a fresh set of eyes sometimes ends up snowballing into much more, especially as you consult with others. It's the 10%, the very precious, unique and valuable 10% that only you can give. You are not compelled to do this out of want or because you can. No. Under the blues skies, it is what you owe. Release the 10.

GODMOTHER

My godparents lived two doors away from my parents' house. They probably agreed to be godparents because my mother was best friends with my godmother. I had little contact with them other than playing with their youngest son, alongside the other sixty odd kids who lived on our block. When I saw the mama's boy we knew as a kid a few years ago at his dad's wake and funeral after an absence of more than half a century, he'd grown into a giant. I remember a wonderful first communion cake Godmother made in the shape of a lamb, covered with coconut flakes to simulate lambswool. I've loved coconut ever since. In any case, Godmother had an elder son who became a lawyer, as well as a beautiful daughter as her middle child. The story I remember from my mother is that backing out of a driveway on Walkley Road while picking her daughter up from piano lessons, my Godmother was hit broadside by a drunk driver. My godparent's daughter was killed. The whole street became somber, and Godmother retreated... though she and Ma still managed to connect over tea most afternoons. Years later, Ma was distraught because it turned out that, since the accident, Godmother had been nursing a secret vodka addiction. According to ma, confronted by her family, it was discovered she had cancer and had a matter of days or weeks to live. Ma was heartbroken. I send them all blessings of power and love. Condolences, we exist in each other.

THE PAIN STOPS HERE

How widely can you apply this powerful phrase? Let me explain how I came to know about it in the first place by providing its context. I have a friend whose family was struck by a freak tragedy and lost one of their children. They were understandably torn apart. No one ever gets over the death of a child. His wife was distraught to no end, and his remaining kids questioned how they might carry on without their missing sibling. My friend himself was in comparable pain, yet as the days dragged on, he saw what was happening to his family. He called a meeting and asked each of them to express their sadness and outrage and promised they would be supported. The caveat he added was that once they did this, they were going to put this behind them and go about their lives in honour of their fallen loved one. He told them clearly, THE PAIN STOPS HERE. And so that is what they did. It wasn't easy, but it had to be done he told me. He and his wife managed to carry on and their remaining children grew up and became parents in their own right. I'm grateful to this brave man for sharing his experience with me. His declaration is one of those courageous acts we rarely encounter, and a lesson I've applied widely. I send them all blessings of power and love in profound gratitude.

RESISTANCE

For a dozen years or so, I worked in paid circulation for the newspaper industry, working myself up from crew manager to senior VP Canada. At one point, I had more than 150 reps and 15 managers reporting to me in seven cities for a dozen newspaper clients. There was plenty of opportunity to coach, counsel, mentor, and advise, and I think I'd still be doing it today if the digital era hadn't done the print newspapers a serious blow. My income shrank each year starting in 2010, and finally in 2015, I felt I had to leave, albeit reluctantly. So, I sold energy for a few years to businesses and farms. After teaching sales for a decade, I had to move from manager to sales rep to earn a living. I remember one time I met with the owner of a shoe store with a half dozen locations. Not high volume but still a nice account. I couldn't close him; he'd been through the process before with a different company. What was interesting was that as I made my way back to my vehicle, I walked past a Dairy Queen store, notorious energy hogs, with all the freezers and fridges and what not. I caught myself RESISTING going in and walking past. I put on the brakes, reset my body and mind, and turned right around and went in. I met the owner Joe, and it turned out he had three locations. He was trying to figure out how to get his freezers out without taking out the windows because they had been installed before the windows were put in and needed replacing. I used the secret of rapport and spent an hour with him, mostly talking about how to manage staff. He picked my brains, and I gained confidence. I didn't sign him up, but what I did was refuse to walk away from resistance again. I used that mindset to sign up farms and businesses all over Eastern Ontario, never looking back. Eventually, I left the business, but that lesson in overcoming resistance re-established a strong belief in myself that I could do anything.

RAPPORT SECRET

In addition to the newspaper industry, I got my start selling magazines door to door in the 1970s. I did other things but later ran big sales teams all over Southern Ontario selling flowers at the door, doing well until debit cards became popular. We used to run a continuous ad for all three jobs to hire and replace staff because the turnover was high. It forced me to become a better manager to retain my staff. I looked after them and taught them plenty. When I left newspapers in 2015, I got hundreds of thankful messages from old reps when I posted it on social media. One of the things I taught was the secret to rapport. I realized the secret by watching myself and then noting what worked and sharing that with my reps over the years. Through repetition, I was able to boil it down to two parts of the same factor. To apply it as I teach it requires that you shed all neediness, insecurity, and expectations. You will soon see why you must decide to BE this person. The secret to building INSTANT RAPPORT with people is to treat them AS IF you have ALWAYS known them while assuming YOU ALWAYS WILL.

That's it. But you must believe it to pull it off because it's no small thing. You must come from THAT place inside you. Do not give yourself a moment to think anything or anyway else. When you look into their eyes, you see someone familiar. You see their history, and you see them yesterday and today and tomorrow and long into the future just by glancing at a face. They must see this in your eyes in return. Because you see yourself in them, you share humanity, history, joy and pain. That is a critical factor: authenticity. Sweep your side of the street. In that moment, you are pure of heart. Your words and affect and body language must be congruent. Failure to be real instils distrust. You have people in your life you have always known. Perhaps it's siblings, parents, children, long-time friends. What does it feel like to interact with them? Easy? Good. Make it exactly like that with everyone. No exceptions.

DAD

One of the things the Grant-Gluek Harvard-Boston study found was that men without warm maternal relations had a four-fold increase in dementia at the end of their lives. Born in the depression era of the last century to a WWI veteran turned advertising executive (Mad Men style) and his pretty wife, my dad was the youngest of four with three older sisters. Unfortunately, my grandfather probably developed what we would now call PTSD and turned on his family. In the year before my sisters put my father in care, Dad told me his first memory. He was about fours years of age, sitting outside his shared bedroom on the top step of the stairs to the second floor. He could hear his father hitting his mother in the kitchen below, angrily shouting at her. When he told me, in some ways he re-enacted the moment, becoming a four-year-old at age eighty-seven. Clenching his fists, he told me of his frustration and how he wanted to go down and intervene but was too scared, so he sat there immobilized with fear. His dad was later committed to an institution, while she moved in with her mother.

Dad was raised there in Halifax, with three sisters, Mom and his Grandma. His mother had lost her own father in the Great Halifax Explosion of 1917 and searched for him for days in a snowstorm before finding out he'd been killed. My grandfather had lost two older sisters to fever as a boy, hearing them call to each other in the night before finding them dead in the morning. His mother bled to death at age forty trying to deliver twins. He was shot earlier in the war and gave up the ground to become a pilot. He crashed at the end of the war and stayed in England rehabilitating a head injury until 1920. Meanwhile his father's horse and buggy were hit by a train in the dark one night, and his dad was killed.

Granddad finally reconciled with his wife in the 1960s, and when he came over to visit when I was a boy, he checked my father's head for "Wallace corners" to ascertain if his son was his. Had they existed, a DNA test would have been unnecessary as they were so alike. My father told me many times that he wished he would have decked his dad that day in the driveway, tensing up each time. That's what his mother and father had been fighting about when my Dad was four, his paternity, and his father disowned him the rest of his days. Writing for his own nine children later, Dad said he loved his parents, but both of them broke his heart. When my grandfather died aged 98, my father held his hand right to the last second, hoping for a reconciliation. None came. My father himself bounced between tyrant and weakling abdicator most of my childhood and very occasionally rose to manifest his king energy. Taking a medical discharge from the Navy with manic-depression, he in many ways remained that immobilized four-year-old boy sitting at the top of the stairs to the very end. Four years after Ma died and following a tragic two-year decline, dementia finally got him.

MY EPIPHANY

Lying on a couch mid-day, when I should probably have been gainfully employed, my broken arm in a cast from where I had blocked the second blow to my head from a baseball hat, after one from behind knocked me down and nearly out. Nurturing still the collapsed lung and hole through my chest where I had been subsequently shot by a cross bow and pinned to the cupboard door in a drug dealer's kitchen—while crack cooked on the stove. The chest hole, plugged with a finger after pulling out the arrow, hissing with the sound of my escaping life, was healing well. The shoulder-to-hand cast made shooting dope a real chore. The drainage bag taped to my side made me feel vulnerable, as if my condition were chronic instead of temporary. Lying there, contemplating my life, I spotted my son crawling into the room.

This beautiful little boy, all blue eyes and blond-haired perfection, spied me in my abandoned position. He trundled over on all fours with an enthusiasm I couldn't help noticing, more so against the backdrop of my black mood and darkened life. He sought to take up his usual spot by clumsily standing on two unsteady feet, gripping my shirt to gain traction, and pulling himself up onto my belly. Once there, he turned himself around and sat perched on his daddy. He watched TV with me, sucking his thumb. I let my gaze wander back and forth from the TV to him, finally settling on him.

I realized looking at his profile, the wisps of blond curls framing his white skin and chubby cheeks, he was the only person I knew with no enemies. He had done no harm to anyone. He owed no debt to the world. He wanted nothing but to be loved by his parents. He may have been the only person I knew in that enviable position. His slate was clean. Slowly, like a morning fog lifting from a lake as the sun rises in the sky, it dawned on me. I would have to be a callous and unfeeling individual to leave this little dependent to the unknown. What would greet his future? How would it be defined?

This came to me, verily, the influences I could see: the mercies of single motherhood; of a fatherless existence of possible despair and longing; of sequential suitors using his mom while subjecting him to risk in the pursuit of her body. Before me, the path being contemplated: most assuredly one that I would follow blindly and with determined hate fueling its fire; one which would risk that I'd eventually languish in jail, largely forgotten by his childhood existence. Who did I think I was? To do this, to this little boy, this innocent, the one who depended on me for protection.

He depended on me, HIS protector. It was I, ME, in charge of protecting one little boy. It was my watch. It was my responsibility and mine alone. That word, protection, applied not as some quid pro quo deal made on the street, not as a bargain with chaos, but rather, in service of an innocent. It was a different game. It wasn't something I could duck or pass off on anyone else. No. When he looked at me, we were inextricably linked: I was his father.

That singular thought suddenly dawned on me with all the force and depth of the ages. However, we had gotten to where we were, I had to know that no one else on the planet could replace me in his life. I was it. I'd never felt so needed. Not like this. Everyone knew I would retaliate. It would be done with a finality borne of my position as a thug, as a fearless antisocial living the code. For I was a fool honouring a system of retribution understood only by the street. The whole of the dirty city knew I was coming: the cops, my adversaries, and all those hangers-on who speculated on the when and how. Word was sure to travel on the rounder's underground: Wallace would have to act. No choice here. There was also little likelihood of pulling it off surreptitiously, it was that expected. I was most likely then under surveillance round-the-clock. All phones around me would have been tapped. There may have been microphones in the very room in which I found myself. Cameras would have been aimed at my front door from out there somewhere. I may have to sacrifice it all as if it were a preordained act, a foregone conclusion awaited gleefully by the man who would relish putting me away... forever.

But that day, looking at that little boy, my little boy, his innocence and beauty so plain to see, his need to be loved by only me so great and so obvious, I blinked. Yes, I hesitated. For once, I checked myself. For him, I questioned my reactionary lifestyle and made my first good decision as a father. I decided then and there that if all my life amounted to, in its totality, was to be a successful dad to this little man, then that is the way it had to be. The asshole that shot me would have to wait until another day to die.

I never looked back. And my boy is now a grown man and turned out fine. In fact, after working in newspapers with me here in Canada, he went on a great European adventure in the name of love. He has seen more places than I already. At the end of his visa period, he married his love, just in time to stay in her country. Practical fella, my boy is. Considering I married his mother in a plea to impress a judge and stay out of prison, his situation is an improvement.

My assailant was gunned down in a pool hall some two years later, after threatening to kill a man's kids if he didn't shoot one of his rivals. It was the same M.O. he'd used on me. That person got life. I was free. I went on to school, graduated first in my class, and moved my family several times across the country and back. Alas, my marriage did not last; nevertheless, fatherhood defined me.

And, on or around his 18th birthday, I was busting my son's balls, a lifelong habit he had to get used to. I told him that I was going to forego the estimated hundred and fifty grand it cost me to raise him (I'd read that amount somewhere). My duty to him as a parent was over and whatever help he received from me going forward would be based on our relationship and not from a sense of duty to care for him materialistically any longer. I wanted him to know I had done my job.

He listened earnestly, then smiled, thinking for a moment, and responded: "Dad, Mom gave me clothes to wear, made me great food, and drove me to school and stuff, and I love and appreciate her. But everything I know, I mean, everything I have learned about life, happiness, people, and myself, I have learned from you. So, thanks, Pops. I love you."

And with that, he hugged me and kissed me on both cheeks. Fuhgetaboutit…

THE ENERGY BILL

Let's talk about personality integration. It was Dr. Robert Glover's *No More Mr. Nice Guy* that put me onto dealing with my "piece of shit" shame as a type one nice guy. Firstly, let me point out that to use the term "integration" clearly implies that there exists disintegration in a man.

We must not fear this. This is work most men never do and it costs them. What they find is they are often "hooked" or "triggered" by circumstances and so they learn to avoid them. Or they have motivations they don't understand or acknowledge. This puts him in a weaker position and although this strategy works, it's still a pattern of avoidance and he usually remains dissatisfied.

The problems start early. When a child is forced to align with benefactors over his own instincts at a level beyond his ability to understand, he will cling to acceptance and turn away from parts of himself. Parents use guilt successfully but when that guilt exceeds the child's ability to resolve, he will reluctantly move forward, subjugating himself to his caregiver's will. He is thus forced to stifle and deny a part of himself to avoid the perceived rejection of his parents. This is how shame develops in degrees.

What other choice does the boy have? He relies upon his caregivers for his entire succorance: nurturing, shelter, safety, and the positive regard he craves. The carrot and stick, threat and reward approaches by his caregivers act as a takeaway close, and seed in him a craving for acceptance and unconditional love.

As he grows into adulthood, part of his energy is spent unconsciously holding those denied parts of himself in check, all the while conflicted under this push and pull. This causes confusion, doubt, and a lesser existence.

The psyche holds back some of his talent, for it is indiscriminate in its defense of the soul. The spirit speaks… but is muffled. The yearning is there but is wild, unreconciled and often, steeped in suffering. It's like having a house with an enormous electricity bill. To save power, you turn off lights and switch to fluorescent bulbs and even install energy saving appliances. To no avail, your bill is still too high. Then one day, perhaps when another expensive bill arrives in the mail, you discover an underground cable running from just below the fuses in your power panel to the back wall and towards the direction of an old shed deep in the backyard. It's right on the fence line with the next property and as far as you know, no one ever goes there.

You thought it was empty, none of your business, not yours to deal with, and so, you have avoided it. After enquiring around and establishing that it is fact part of your land, you get the courage to break into the shed. Inside, you are temporarily blinded as you find 1000-watt bulbs, lots of them, running 24/7. It's not a cannabis grow-op so what else could it be? Seeking the source of this power you spot the feed going into the ground towards the direction of the main house. Just as you are saying to yourself, "Holy shit! How long has this been going on?" you spot what looks like an image of your younger self, floating in suspended animation under the intensity of the lights. You recognize him from pictures you have seen of yourself. Bewildered, you suddenly realize he is held in by the energy you yourself have unknowingly been providing all these years...

He responds only to your voice. You can't explain what you do and say for these are as mysterious as the situation itself, but you give yourself over to discovery, determined not to leave the boy behind.

You have a conversation and it's the most important talk you ever have. You listen and reacquaint yourself with him and once you have regained his trust, promise to never leave him again. You gently invite him to come up and into the big house.

He tells you things, and it's as if he's been waiting a long time for the two of you to be reunited and to share his story. You reassure him. He tells you more. You fill in blanks with whatever wisdom you have accumulated, and you realize what you need to do is to reparent him. He's afraid but you persevere and take him wherever you go. He learns to handle new experiences as you defend him.

Slowly but surely, you bring him into your heart and more... ♡ He's not alone anymore, you are there for him and the two of you are fully reunited, and inextricably linked to each other. You have conversations in various circumstances, and he gives his perspective. You acknowledge and lead him from where he is in his confusion and suffering to where you are now with clarity and hope.

You become more powerful. Assured. Capable. Humble. You use power 💪 and love ♡ in service of yourself and others. You create a life of meaning, and finally, you taste... freedom.

Time goes by...

One day you realize you don't carry the boy with you any longer. The shed out back has long been emptied. The lights have been turned off and removed. The power cable was dug up. The splice into the main house disconnected. You appreciate the extra storage space and begin keeping your lawnmower and other tools there.

And you never forget him as you say goodbye. In a sense, the boy has died so the man could live. You are not sad. You are powerful. The two of you have become one. Assimilated, transcended, integrated…

The next energy bill comes in… you find it's considerably less expensive. Now that you control all your own power.

Find the Taming Shame course at this link:

https://services.advisortomen.com/courses/taming-shame

THE BEST OF ME

All of us can remember times where we screwed up. In his song "My Way," Frank Sinatra sang "Regrets? I've had a few…" and although he does it his way, it's those God-awful moments in life that seem to stick with us. Times where we wished we could disappear, be swallowed by the ground beneath us, transported to another dimension. It is our inherent negativity bias, something which helps us stay alive, turning to bite us in the ass with disappointment.

But what of those "other" times? I am referring to moments where you perhaps surprised yourself and walked away from something damn proud at how you handled a challenge. We tend to sweep those away, allowing only a momentary surge of good feeling, before filing the experience permanently under "long forgotten." I say bullshit.

So, here's what you do: take four such experiences and write them down. Cover body, spirit, people and work, or any other category of which you can think. If you can only produce one, that's fine too. Write it down and make it your beacon, a target for what you are capable of and what you must exceed. Look only for these opportunities each day. Beat the best experience you have ever had, where you determined your fate, where it was your talent and disposition that rose to conquer a fear, push through a barrier, or save the moment or even, the day. Each day going forward, be this person and no other. Be only your version of the Best of Me.

TRAUMA TRAP

One of the reason I don't subscribe to the "trauma causes addiction" trope is because it's illogical.

It is a "false cause" to say trauma causes addiction unless you widen your definition of trauma to include "anything that has ever happened to an individual." So... life causes addictions. I get it.

While I sympathize with those who have experienced trauma and count myself among them, I don't see much advantage to following that path. Mostly I agree, but with my own perspective.

Labels are always a judgment call. On the one hand, a label can mean freedom from confusion and isolation and a path forward. Labels can also become a merry-go-round of circular thinking, as in "I am an addict because I have trauma. Why did I relapse? Because I have trauma." ffs.

I cannot think of a less advantageous way to think about it. Here's a couple of examples.

Prematurely born babies often wind up with a nervous system that leans heavily to protection over connection. How are you going to resolve that as an adult? Call it trauma and send them to yoga? Have them do body work to recapture the moment their body was unable to complete its need to shake it out and resolve its fear? Maybe... and cross your fingers...

And if the baby grows up to be a fear-seeker, but otherwise had a good upbringing with better than average parents, is the answer to talk about their "trauma?" I don't think it is.

My son was born with a handful of medical issues. He's been poked and prodded and rushed to hospital more than most kids. He spent his first few months at Sick Kids, came home and had to return, usually by ambulance. Missus has watched him code blue several times while she herself was pushed up against the wall as 25 specialists worked to keep him alive. She definitely had trauma.

As for the boy, he's pretty careful about EVERYTHING but is otherwise, normal. I've been watching him, "trauma informed" as I am. If the compressor went on in the garage while we were in it, he'd run away. It's taken me years to get him used to that. Letting the air out with a big BANG after we are done with the compressor filling up his bike tires, well… he's not managed that yet.

His doctor's visits have been a long process of exposure therapy. If he sees a needle, he will be under the table or hiding in a corner trying to get away. Missus usually brings someone to help. She has gal pals with training in child development. Team Human, and he gets double the love.

She starts prepping him for visits to Children's Hospital a week in advance. I can hear her talk to him in the kitchen from my office, allowing him to ask questions, patiently answering with truth and determination, instilling an agreed upon courage before they go. Missus can care-give like a champ.

It's also cost missus a lot of cheeseburgers in rewards. She bought him a tablet so he can distract himself with playing Roblox to get by. Otherwise, he is a normal little boy and wonderful to a fault. I am getting him to make his bed some mornings. He lets out the chickens and locks them up at night. Often in his underwear and wearing my big rubber boots. Evenings he does this on his own, pleasantly surprised and thankful if I got to them first for him. He's unfailingly polite.

When he has something on his mind he will say, "I have a question…" and wait until he has your attention before proceeding. He's been doing this since he was about six years old. He's nine now. Who says that at nine? I get a kick out of it every time I hear it. Or he will show you something and if your attention wanes for even a split second he will say, "Look! Look!…" before continuing. It makes me smile. I'm watching him carefully for signs of fear seeking and will be there to teach him even more how to regulate and expand his "neuroceptive" ability. Neuroception is your situational awareness filtered through lived experience, a highly personalized "Spidey-sense" for threat assessment.

To counter what I believe his nervous system has learned, I teach him how to connect with others. He's a fearless communicator and though too young for the Big Five, I think he would score high in assertiveness. If a kid like Howie or a child born prematurely developed an addiction, calling it trauma that needs to be "resolved" is less useful. The risk is we compound things, doubling down on an injured and broken status, a self concept which to me risks feeding personal shame. I'm not doing it. Wrong guy.

Better to show them what fear addiction is and how it can manifest as fear seeking.

Better to show them how their nervous systems is wired for protection over connection and can be retrained by experience otherwise.

Better to teach them how to connect... with others, themselves, the world around them...

Better to show them it is Freudian myth to think you must resolve all your emotional problems to make better decisions for yourself today.

Better to teach them how to bring awareness to their tendency to choose fear and instead, make plenty of room to choose confidence.

Better to show them how to defend every bit of earned confidence to live a life of destiny.

That's how you resolve addictions.

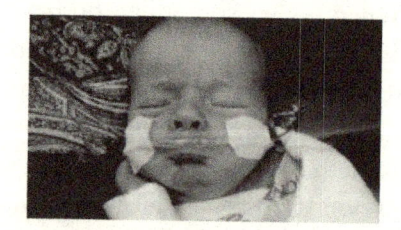

©CHRISTOPHER K WALLACE, 2022, Sipping Fear,
all rights reserved advisortomen.com

Back Page

I cured my insomnia using these, my 12 favourite ways of getting to sleep.

https://services.advisortomen.com/courses/SLEEPCURE

Try my FREE napping advantage course to make your commutes safer

https://services.advisortomen.com/courses/the-napping-advantage-your-self-care-secret-weapon

The Integration Course Taming Shame has been life-changing for hundreds of men

https://services.advisortomen.com/courses/taming-shame

Become your own anxiety expert by taking Anxiety Action here

https://services.advisortomen.com/courses/anxiety-action

Get the House Rules: 12 Ideas for Effective Communication for FREE when you sign up for my newsletter at https://www.advisortomen.com/

©CHRISTOPHER K WALLACE, 2022, Sipping Fear, all rights reserved advisortomen.com

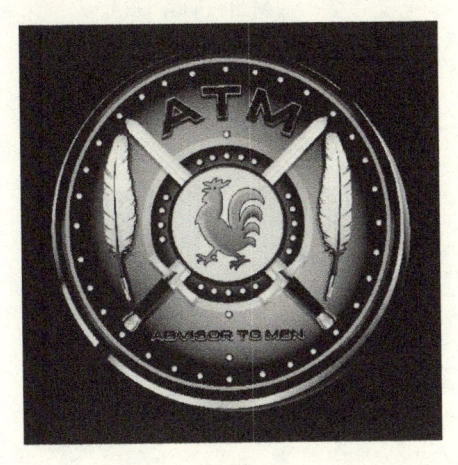

Made in the USA
Las Vegas, NV
13 November 2023